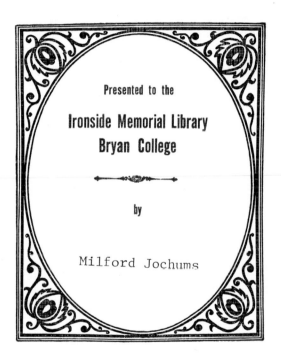

MILTON'S USE OF
DU BARTAS

MILTON'S USE OF
DU BARTAS

BY

GEORGE COFFIN TAYLOR

1968

OCTAGON BOOKS, INC.

New York

Reprinted 1967

by special arrangement with Harvard University Press

OCTAGON BOOKS, INC.
175 Fifth Avenue
New York, N. Y. 10010

Library of Congress Catalog Card Number: 67-18787

Printed in U.S.A. by
NOBLE OFFSET PRINTERS, INC.
NEW YORK 3, N. Y.

To

ELLEN ELMORE TAYLOR

"DIE FRANZOSEN HABEN EINEN POETEN DU BARTAS, DEN SIE GAR NICHT MEHR ODER NUR MIT VERACHTUNG NENNEN."

Kürschner's *Deutsche National-Literatur*,
"Goethe Werke," vol. 29, p. 162 f.

Preface

TO THE average reader of Milton, Du Bartas is merely a name signifying nothing. To many students of the Renaissance it suggests the most pedestrian epic of that period. To Milton scholars it generally calls to mind a rather doubtful and negligible influence upon Milton's juvenile poems, an influence, moreover, which he might well have counted himself happy to outgrow. Among the great authorities on Milton, none is to be found who maintains that Du Bartas is of major importance as an immediate and direct source of his great epic, *Paradise Lost*. This book ventures to establish beyond dispute that no other work of the Renaissance had a more important and definite influence on *Paradise Lost* than Sylvester's translation of Du Bartas. If the conclusions of this study prove to be sound, the indirect influence of Du Bartas upon English literature through Milton's imitators is obviously immense.

For aid in the preparation of the manuscript my thanks are due to Professor George Lyman Kittredge in a multitude of particulars. Over a period of years I have repeatedly relied upon his advice and judgment in connection with this work. I wish to thank also the authorities of the University of North Carolina, whose financial aid, through the Kenan Endowment Fund, the Smith Research Fund, and the Library, has made it possible for me to complete this work. Thanks are due also to the Harvard College Library, which has extended to me invaluable aid. I wish to thank also Professors C. F. Tucker Brooke and Chauncey B. Tinker for extending to me the use of the Yale Library.

G. C. T.

CHAPEL HILL, NORTH CAROLINA
April 1, 1934

Contents

Introduction

NO AUTHORITY on Milton has ever acknowledged in any sense adequately the importance and extent of the use which Milton made of Du Bartas in writing *Paradise Lost*. Perhaps because the discussion of Du Bartas-Milton relations, which began one hundred and eighty-four years ago with William Lauder's *An Essay on Milton's Use and Imitation of the Moderns in his Paradise Lost* (1750), was conceived in hatred by a forger,[1] scholars ever since have labored under a misapprehension as to the significance of the indebtedness of *Paradise Lost* to the translation of *La Sepmaine ov Creation*, entitled *Du Bartas His Divine Weekes and Workes*, not published in complete collected form until 1608.[2] In order to correct this misapprehension I shall find it necessary to call attention repeatedly to possible inaccuracies in the conclusions of many of the most outstanding recent investigations that seek to establish relationships between Milton and individual authors or provinces of literature. I wish to emphasize all the more strongly that this book is not in any sense an attack on that splendid movement in Milton scholarship which, inaugurated some sixteen years ago by Greenlaw and Saurat, and aided and further developed by Gilbert, Miss Nicolson, E. N. S. Thompson, Larson, Fletcher, Miss Hartwell, and others, has succeeded in bringing about a veritable Renaissance of Milton study, and in opening up fresh and stimulating approaches to his major works. Thanks to these scholars, the present-day reader no longer accepts Raleigh's impression of *Paradise Lost* as "a monument to

1. The *spirit* of Lauder's interpretations was that of one demented. His facts were important, particularly in view of trends of Milton scholarship since 1917. See the Reverend John Todd, *The Poetical Works of John Milton*, London, 1842, notes, for Lauder's citations and for other Du Bartas references.

2. See W. R. Abbot's discovery, p. 7, note 1, of this study.

dead ideas," but finds instead running through that wonderful work of art veins of rich and vital thought invisible to the average student of the generations preceding. This study seeks to push further forward the recent researches by availing itself of bodies of literature absolutely necessary to the clarification of the entire field of study.

By a singular accident, *The Hexaemeral Literature*, by F. E. Robbins, the most valuable study throwing light on those themes in *Paradise Lost* which investigators since 1917 have been seeking to trace in other authors, though published in 1912, has not been mentioned by any of them.[1] The recent investigators of Milton's readings have failed also to reckon with the Mirrour Literature of the Middle Ages and the Renaissance (represented, for example, by *L'Image du Monde* written in 1245 by Maitre Gossouin, translated by Caxton in 1497, and represented as late as the seventeenth century by Swan's *Speculum* of 1635), involving most comprehensively almost all of the themes investigated by scholars recently. These two genres, the Hexaemeral and Mirrour literatures, finally grew to such proportions as to include the treatment of almost every kind of special and general information available in their respective periods, with particular emphasis on science and pseudo-science. They make it possible to trace the origin and development of an immense number of ideas,[2] of blocks of literary material and of literary forms, which recent scholars have sought to trace in this or that particular work by way of throwing light on

1. Not cited by either D. H. Stevens or H. F. Fletcher in their recent valuable bibliographical contributions: *Reference Guide to Milton*, Chicago, 1930; *Contributions to a Milton Bibliography*, Urbana, Illinois, 1931.

2. A few of these themes are: God, His nature and attributes, His Son or The Word as distinguished from God and from Christ, the Angels and their Functions, the origin of Matter, Chaos, origins of Vegetable and Animal life, the origin of man, Adam's intellectual perfection, his Fall, the results of his Fall on himself and on the Universe, the method of his reinstatement to his original state or to a better state through Christ.

the forms they assume in *Paradise Lost*. They make it possible to show also that most of these ideas had become veritable commonplaces not simply of the Renaissance but of the Dark Ages as well.

Finally, paradoxical as it may appear, this book will maintain that there is one work, that of Du Bartas, in which the Hexaemeral and Mirrour literatures converge, and through which the great body of these conventional commonplaces found their way into *Paradise Lost*. To contend that Du Bartas is the only force in shaping the ideas, the blocks of material, the structure of this material or the spirit of its interpretation, would be unwise in view of the vast bodies of literature in which they are commonplaces and in view of the man Milton, better equipped than any other English poet to explore these by-paths of the Middle Ages and the Renaissance. It has long been known that Milton consulted special works on all of the themes he developed. This study, indeed, will assist in disclosing that *Paradise Lost* includes the gradual accumulation of a bewildering number of conventional ideas and conventional expressions, much as has been shown to be the case with *Lycidas* in the matter of the conventions of the pastoral dirges.[1] It will maintain, nevertheless, that, as throwing light on the form of these themes in *Paradise Lost*, *The Divine Weekes* is altogether the most important single book of the Renaissance; that Milton resorted to it early and late, as so many others were doing, as the best book on universal knowledge in poetical form accessible in his day — to such an extent, indeed, as to make it hardly an exaggeration to call it Milton's quarry.

This study will offer evidence enough to convince scholars of the amazing neglect of Du Bartas in connection with Milton studies. It should enable scholars and general readers to follow Milton in

1. Norlin, *The Conventions of the Pastoral Elegy, American Journal of Philology*, XXXII, (1911) 294 ff.; Hanford, *The Pastoral Elegy and Milton's Lycidas, P.M.L.A.*, xxv (1910), 403 ff.

his workshop transmuting his materials on a grand scale under our very eyes through stages of artistry fascinating and amazing. Thus it will appear in what a hazy sense scholars have used the term "modernity" in regard to Milton, since this modernity is largely to be accounted for by his remarkable selection of those aspects of thought and feeling of the commentators on Genesis, of the great Church Fathers, and of other Medieval and Renaissance writers, which we rather too arrogantly term modern. Yet this study will prove but a vain and empty thing if it fails to enlarge our scholarly vision of Milton's marvelous capacity for absorbing material and subjecting it to those assimilative and sublimating processes which brought into being the miracle of *Paradise Lost*. It is difficult to get away from the words of Samuel Johnson in any connection. He justified the earliest of English studies of the sources of Milton in words which, however unhappily associated at the time with Lauder, now prove to be singularly appropriate. They afford, he says, "a retrospection of the progress of this mighty genius in the construction of his work; a view of the fabric gradually rising perhaps from small beginnings." [1]

1. Lauder, *An Essay on Milton's Use and Imitation of the Moderns in his Paradise Lost*, 1750, Preface.

Chapter I

MODERN MISCONCEPTIONS
OF MILTON–DU BARTAS RELATIONS

R EPRESENTATIVE conclusions of the authorities will illustrate how all are prone to minimize the debt of Milton
to Du Bartas. When William Lauder in 1750 wrote in
malice *An Essay on Milton's Use and Imitation of the Moderns in
his Paradise Lost*, the authorities on Milton sprang to his defense
and proved Lauder to be, like Collier, a forger.[1] From that time
until to-day scholarship has continued to perpetuate the impression which arose out of the heat of that furious controversy which
cleared Milton from the charge of dishonesty. Even fifty years
after Lauder's attack, Charles Dunster's able *Considerations on
Milton's Early Reading and the Prima Stamina of his Paradise
Lost*, which points out an immense number of verbal similarities
between Du Bartas and Milton, particularly in the Minor Poems,
was thought to indicate merely "a general obligation"[2] on
Milton's part.

The statements of the acknowledged authorities on Milton in
recent works illustrate the extraordinary tenacity of tradition in
regard to the impression that Milton's indebtedness to Du Bartas
is uncertain, general, and insignificant. The statement of A. H.
Upham[3] is probably the best known and most generally accepted.
After reviewing the history of Du Bartas-Milton studies, he says:

1. J. W. Good, *Studies in the Milton Tradition*, 1915, pp. 185–191.
2. *Monthly Mirror*, x (1800), 155–156.
3. *The French Influence in English Literature*, 1908, pp. 215–216.

The question of Milton's relations to Du Bartas was one of great importance to certain scholars of a century ago, but of late it has almost disappeared from view. The citations and parallels brought out by this scholarship were of no particular value. . . . The whole question lies slightly outside the scope of this study, and at best offers little more than the thread of probability indicated above. By the time of England's civil strife, literary influences such as Du Bartas and Sylvester represented had become so various and complicated that it is next to impossible to point out definite instances of dependence.

Sir Sidney Lee,[1] whose statement is about as well known to students of Anglo-French relations as Upham's, is not aware of any important debt of *Paradise Lost* to Du Bartas, and leaves the matter with the cloudy phrase, "the degree of the relation is open to doubt." E. N. S. Thompson,[2] the leading Milton bibliographer previous to 1930, in perhaps the most able and comprehensive running comment ever written on all the sources of Milton says: "Though one grants willingly that Milton probably knew *The Divine Weekes and Workes* in boyhood, it is impossible to believe that a poem so formless and inartistic had any vital influence upon him. Sylvester need not even be credited with having led Milton to choose a Biblical theme." When Raleigh[3] comes to consider Du Bartas, he refers only to "the list of human diseases and maladies suggested perhaps by Du Bartas." Moody[4] says of Du Bartas and of many other suggested sources of *Paradise Lost*, "We may put [them] aside as exhibiting vague, slight, or merely verbal resemblances. A few, however, remain, which are so closely connected with Milton's work that some consideration of them is imperative." Du Bartas is not among Moody's "a few." Verity[5] selects, among all the sources in the field, Grotius, Andreini, Vondel, the Cædmon Paraphrase, and remarks, "These then are the four possible 'sources' of *Paradise Lost* seemingly most de-

---

1. *The French Renaissance in England*, 1910, p. 355.
2. *Essays on Milton*, 1914, p. 164.   3. *Milton*, 1900, p. 237.
4. *The Complete Poetical Works of John Milton*, pp. 93–94.
5. *Paradise Lost*, 1921, Introd., pp. xlviii–lvi.

serving of mention," adding "Finally, we must not forget Sylvester." Greenlaw, though admitting that Du Bartas, among other encyclopedic works, in a general way influenced Spenser and Milton,[1] in his two articles on Spenser's influence on Milton[2] does not concede to Du Bartas a single instance of direct influence such as he maintained in the case of Spenser. Tillyard[3] is somewhat stronger in his statement as to indebtedness, but he continues the traditional emphasis upon Du Bartas in the Minor Poems, referring, without offering new evidence, to only a general influence upon *Paradise Lost*. Hanford in the most recent of all statements on the subject follows the tradition also. In considering Book VII of *Paradise Lost*, he refers to the account of the Creation, "a theme," says Hanford,[4] "which Milton pursues with eagerness after the *general* precedent of such independent Biblical poems as Du Bartas' *La Sepmaine* and Tasso's *Il Mondo Creato*." (Italics mine.) Referring later to Milton's account of the Creation, Hanford is particularly careful to say that Sylvester's translation "may be counted, *though vaguely*, as helping to determine Milton's predisposition to the writing of a didactical Biblical poem of cyclopedic scope."[5] In short, Milton scholars seem fairly uniform in their agreement upon some such theory as that just quoted from Upham: "Literary influences . . . had become so various and complicated that it is next to impossible to point out definite instances of dependence." Not since William Lauder launched the Du Bartas-Milton movement in English scholarship in 1750 has anyone in England or America until within the last five years presented any appreciable body of evidence in substantiation of the

1. *The New Science and English Literature in the Seventeenth Century, The Johns Hopkins Alumni Magazine*, XIII (1925), 353 ff.
2. *Studies in Philology*, XIV (1917), 196 ff.; XVII (1920), 320 ff.
3. *Milton*, 1930, pp. 8, 9, 11, 16.
4. James Holly Hanford, *A Milton Handbook* (revised) 1933, p. 186.
5. The same, p. 228. Italics mine.

direct influence of Du Bartas on *Paradise Lost*. The only efforts
made by English or American scholarship to assemble such evidence are those of Haight [1] and Candy,[2] both of whom offer a few
evidences of verbal borrowings of decided value. Only one writer
has come out recently advocating Du Bartas as influencing Milton.
J. W. Mackail [3] adds little if any new evidence, but asserts a
heavy debt on Milton's part in such fashion as to construct a rhetorical antithesis worthy of Macauley: "In the whole range of
Jacobean poetry, the work to which Milton has most recourse is a
second rate translation of a second rate original, Sylvester's version of the Sepmaine of Du Bartas." In Germany Wilhelm
Münch [4] assembles ten or twelve verbal parallels of interest suggesting a reminiscent influence. And Alfred Stern [5] in the great
German work on Milton cites no parallels but stresses the important influence of Du Bartas on the juvenile poems. In Belgium, also,
Thibaut de Maisieres [6] presents no resemblances, suggests that
they are easy to detect, and concludes "collationner les deux
textes, phrase par phrase, ainsi que l'a fait Lauder, est une besogne
assez stérile." In France two studies of Du Bartas assemble important groups of similarities between Du Bartas and Milton.
Pellissier [7] rightly calls attention to similarities as to Satan's entrance into Paradise, his temptation of Eve, the list of diseases,
the brooding of the Holy Spirit over chaos, and other more
general similarities, concluding, "Mais la langue et le goût de du
Bartas le mettent tellement audessous de Milton qu'on éprouve
quelque scrupule à la comparer." [8] As in the case of those writing

---

1. *The Divine Weeks of Joshua Sylvester*, Waukesha, Wisconsin, 1908, pp. 22 ff.
2. *Milton's Early Readings of Sylvester, Notes and Queries*, CLVIII (1930), 93 ff.
3. *The Springs of Helicon*, 1909, pp. 195, 196.
4. *Die Enstehung des Verlorenen Paradieses*, Cleve (1874), pp. 24 ff.
5. *Milton und Seine Zeit*, Leipzig (1876), I, pp. 38 ff.
6 *Les Poèmes inspirés du Début de la Genèse à l'Epoque de la Renaissance* (Louvain)
1931, pp. 115 ff.   7. *La Vie et les Œuvres de Du Bartas*, Paris, 1883, pp. 267 ff.
8. The same, p. 256.

in England and America, the force of tradition is too strong also for Ashton, who, after assembling valuable data, reaches negative conclusions, emphasizing the "general" nature of the debt of Milton to Du Bartas.[1] Thus, three hundred years after *La Semaine* was completely translated into English by Sylvester, Upham in America and Ashton[2] in France come to virtually the same conclusion as to its relations to *Paradise Lost*:

A tout prendre, l'influence de Sylvester sur le fond comme sur la forme de l'œuvre la plus considérable de Milton, nous paraît si lointaine, si souvent incertaine, que nous nous demandons où se trouvent les "nombreuses et belles pensées" qu'il aurait dérobées à son prédécesseur. La carrière de pleine maturité de Milton est bien indépendante des influences que nous avons admises en ce qui concerne ses œuvres de jeunesse.

Certains critiques, se refusant à admettre toute influence directe de l'œuvre de Du Bartas, seraient disposés à convenir que ce fut ce poème qui ouvrit à Milton les perspectives de la poésie sacrée.

En parlant de l'œuvre de Du Bartas, envisagée dans son ensemble, nous avons fait ressortir l'influence qu'elle avait pu exercer sur l'orientation de Milton vers la poésie sacrée. Mais il ne faut pas oublier que tout poussait Milton vers ce genre littéraire: le milieu dans lequel il était né, son éducation, l'époque où il a vécu, son caractère. Il ne convient donc pas d'exagérer outre mesure le rôle de Du Bartas. Milton a lu la traduction de Du Bartas comme il a lu beaucoup d'œuvres de même nature, parce qu'il y trouvait exprimées des idées qui lui souriaient déjà et qui, par la pente naturelle de son esprit, devaient devenir chez lui des convictions fermes; mais ce n'est point d'ailleurs à cette traduction plus qu'à toute autre œuvre profane, qu'il faut attribuer le mérite d'avoir fait de Milton un des plus grands poètes sacrés.

---

1. The French attitude towards the entire matter has been amazing. Du Bartas has never been edited by that nation in the modern sense of an edition. The writer called this to the attention of the English and Romance Departments of the University of North Carolina in 1925, with the result that a complete edition of the French text under the able editorship of Urban T. Holmes, J. C. Lyons, and R. W. Linker is now being published by the University of North Carolina Press. This indifference to the French text is only equalled by the fact that, in spite of the valuable contribution of Grosart's modern edition of Sylvester's translation, some twenty-five references to the date of the complete translation by English, American, German, and French authorities are all erroneous. It was not until recently that the date was settled as 1608 (W. R. Abbot, *Studies in the Influence of Du Bartas in England, 1584-1641*. MS. dissertation, University of North Carolina, 1931).

2. *Du Bartas en Angleterre*, Paris, 1908, pp. 304-305.

These representative statements of representative Milton scholars indicate that tradition in English scholarship is clearly against conceding that the relation of Milton to Du Bartas in *Paradise Lost* is of any importance. Scholars seem also to agree that the very nature of the problem renders it incapable of a definite solution.

Practically all the leading Milton scholars in the field to-day realize this difficulty even when seeking most zealously to discover in this or that piece of literature new evidences of possible Milton connections. Greenlaw [1] has ably stated the dangers that beset the source-hunter in this field, but attempts to establish definite borrowings from Spenser notwithstanding. Saurat,[2] even when maintaining that the most important "philosophical" idea in *Paradise Lost* was known to Milton in the *Zohar*, admits the possibility of Milton's having observed it elsewhere. Miss Nicolson is particularly careful to say "less with a desire to establish actual borrowing on the part of Milton than to indicate typically Cabbalistic strains in Paradise Lost." [3] Larson [4] is also aware of the danger of pressing too far the claim of direct relationship between Milton and Servetus. Gilbert [5] makes no claim for an actual first-hand acquaintance of Milton with the Medieval drama. All of these scholars display a wholesome regard for the extraordinary vastness and complexity of the field of sources involved in the problem of discussing the ideas and systems of thought they are seeking to investigate in *Paradise Lost*, though most of them at times attempt to mass their evidence in such a way as to suggest how Milton may have actually borrowed.

In the face of these two sets of facts, then, — the strong tide of

1. *Spenser's Influence on Paradise Lost, Studies in Philology*, xvii (1920), 320 ff.
2. *Milton: Man and Thinker*, 1925, p. 289.
3. *Milton and The Conjectura Cabbalistica, Philological Quarterly*, vi (1927), 2; see also *Studies in Philology*, xxii (1926), 452.
4. *Milton and Servetus, P.M.L.A.*, xli (1926), 891.
5. *Milton and the Mysteries, Studies in Philology*, xvii (1920), 147 ff.

opinion against Du Bartas, and the realization by all authorities of the complexity of the problem, — and in the face, moreover, of Milton's failure to refer to Du Bartas by name, although he mentions six thousand authors,[1] it will perhaps seem incautious on the part of the present study to make the claim that Du Bartas had an immense effect upon *Paradise Lost*, not only in a general but in a most direct and immediate manner. That, however, is precisely what the present study undertakes to do. A contention departing so radically from the received tradition will necessarily have to be supported by evidence of the most convincing nature. The nature of that evidence, the method of its presentation, step by step, will therefore be described at this point, with a view to clarification and making it more easily possible for the critic to subject it to a more thoroughgoing analysis if he sees fit to do so.

This study will maintain that, if there is any one work which constitutes the main force in the Renaissance determining the nature of the materials of *Paradise Lost* investigated by scholars during the last two decades, in regard to their substance, their exact form of expression, and their arrangement or structure, that book is Sylvester's. This it will attempt to do with the aid of material not hitherto employed. The first of these is the dissertation already briefly referred to in the Introduction, which, probably because it lay in the field of the classics, has entirely escaped the notice of all Milton investigators and bibliographers alike. This is the work of Frank Egleston Robbins, *The Hexaemeral Literature, A Study of the Greek and Latin Commentaries on Genesis*, published by the University of Chicago in 1912, thus anticipating by some five years the recent American movement in Milton scholarship. It is hardly possible to overestimate the importance of Robbins' study of the Hexaemeral Literature in relation to that movement. Practically every significant study of sources, including and fol-

1. Allan H. Gilbert's MS. notes.

lowing the work of Greenlaw and Saurat, extending through the researches of Miss Nicolson, M. A. Larson, and E. C. Baldwin, and even through that exceedingly valuable Milton investigation *Milton's Rabbinical Readings* by H. F. Fletcher, will have to be reconsidered with Robbins' results at hand. He sheds light on the entire problem of Milton in relation to the new sources investigated by these scholars. Sometimes in a mere footnote he anticipates an entire article devoted to the study of one of Milton's sources. In short, Robbins traces back through the Greek and Latin Commentaries on Genesis almost literally to the year 1 of the Christian era the great majority of the motives and themes which have been the main consideration of Milton scholars since 1917, in such fashion as to render inevitable the conclusion that they are for the most part the commonplaces not only of the Renaissance, as has been in part suggested and surmised, but of the Middle and Dark Ages as well.

That scholars have been investigating to a very considerable extent the commonplaces of the age becomes apparent also in connection with a province of Medieval and Renaissance literature not studied in its proper relation to that main stream of Renaissance epic material which finally culminated in *Paradise Lost*. I refer to those very popular books of the Middle Ages which would pass to-day under some such title as *What Everybody Ought To Know,* familiar to scholars under several names, but best known perhaps in England as Mirrour Literature. Such, for example, are Caxton's *Mirrour of the World* [1] (1497), *Batman on Bathalome* (1582), Swan's *Speculum* (1629, 1635), and Gossouin's *L'Image du Monde* (1245), the original of Caxton's *Mirrour*. The numerous works cited in the next chapter will make clear the extraordinary similarity of themes common to these compendiums of knowledge, not only with reference to the ordinary themes arising early out of

1. E.E.T.S. Extra Series, cx.

the comment on Genesis but with reference also to their inclusion on an enormous scale of all pseudo-scientific and scientific knowledge. There are lists and comments stretching out to the crack of doom, of animals, fishes, trees, herbs (enough to deserve the name of herbals),[1] precious stones (long enough to be called lapidaries), and lists of diseases and the passions. There are lists also of the phenomena of nature, such as hail and snow, with an incessant inquiry into causes. These are comprehended in Du Bartas, still on an enormous scale. On a very much reduced scale they appear in Milton, but they still appear *as lists*, and, as will be noticed in the chapters that follow, many of them in such language as to leave no room for doubt that their nature is in part determined by Du Bartas.

Finally, the Genesis genre fused also with the chronicle literatures. As Robbins says,[2] "There should be mentioned those short accounts of the creation which some of the chroniclers prefixed to their works. Josephus begins his treatise on Jewish antiquities thus as did Sextus Julius Africanus who wrote at the beginning of the third century, and the practise was common among the Byzantine chroniclers." On an enormously extended scale Du Bartas follows his commentary on Genesis material with the wanderings and battles of Jewish history. Material similar but much reduced and beautifully synthesized and sublimated by Milton's artistry makes its way into Books xi and xii of *Paradise Lost*. How common it was for English chroniclers to prefix comments on Genesis to these chronicles it would be interesting to investigate. Walter Raleigh does this in his *History of the World*,[3] and Grafton's *Abridgment* begins with the statement that "Adam was learned in all the liberal arts and sciences."

1. See Hazel A. Stevenson's MS. dissertation, *Herbal Lore as Reflected in the Works of the Major Elizabethan Poets and Dramatists*, University of North Carolina, 1930.
2. *The Hexaemeral Literature*, 1912, p. 37.
3. See Robbins, *The Hexaemeral Literature*, 1912, p. 102.

In order, therefore, to simplify an exceedingly complex problem and to make certain beyond doubt the commonplace nature of much of the material of *Paradise Lost* investigated in recent years, the following chapter enumerates some sixty topics referred to by scholars as evidence of relationship between Milton and individual authors or individual works, in each case indicating in a footnote the varied and common types of Medieval and Renaissance works in which these ideas occur.   Then, with apparent inconsistency, having demonstrated the hazardousness of venturing a statement of the influence of individual authors or individual works on *Paradise Lost* by reason of the fact that practically every theme of any importance in it had become the common property for literary exercises of the writers of Milton's age and the ages preceding, this study will proceed to demonstrate the very heavy indebtedness of Milton in regard to these very matters to one author, Du Bartas, and to his one work, *La Sepmaine*, as rendered by Sylvester in his translation, *The Divine Weekes and Workes*.[1]   The logic of this apparent lack of logic is to be explained as follows: Whereas only a few of these sixty odd themes have been cited as appearing in this or that author investigated by scholars, virtually all of them appear in Du Bartas and in Milton, as the first citation in each footnote makes clear. The study of these two provinces of Medieval and Renaissance literature, — the one, the Greek and Latin Commentaries on Genesis, running uninterruptedly from Philo Judaeus (A.D. *ca.* 40) to Milton's Christian Doctrine and beyond; the other, the Mirrour or Speculum Literature, represented by Gossouin's *L'Image du Monde*, 1245, translated by Caxton in 1497, or Swan's *Speculum*, 1629, — shows that these two genres, after absorbing all knowledge, theological, profane, and pseudo-scientific, converged in Du Bartas. They converged in no such manner in

---

1. *Du Bartas His Divine Weekes and Workes* by Joshua Sylvester, Gent., London 1641. This edition is more accessible to scholars than the expensive, rare edition of Grosart.

any other epic.[1] Their outcroppings in Milton are so similar in hundreds of details of thought and expression to their outcroppings in Du Bartas that only one conclusion seems possible, and that is that Du Bartas, more than any other writer of the Renaissance, is responsible for their appearance in *Paradise Lost*.

Of course it is open to anyone who wishes to believe it, to maintain that Milton, in addition to what he is already known to have read, — a body of literature greater and more varied than any other English poet up to his time, — read also each one of the individual authors and writings recently cited as his sources. His many references to the Church Fathers in his prose works make it certain that he consulted them often on points which interested him.[2]

It is certainly not my intention to emphasize Milton's debt to Du Bartas to the exclusion of his debt to others. That on certain matters common to Du Bartas and *Paradise Lost* he consulted, as suited his purpose, St. Augustine, Spenser, Sir Henry More, Servetus, and some of the rabbinical readings noticed by Fletcher, this study does not deny. Miss Hartwell[3] has shown that beyond any doubt Milton consulted Lactantius. And how anyone can read Grotius' *Adamus Exul*[4] or Vondel without concluding that Milton had read and liked them, it is impossible for me to comprehend. But it seems only natural to conclude that Milton got the greatest amount of his heterogeneous material from the most heterogeneous of all the epics he had read, — heterogeneous both

1. Tasso's *Mondo Creato*, as will be observed in the footnotes to Chapter II, has a great number. This work was written under the influence of Du Bartas' *Sepmaine*, and is deserving of study in relation to *Paradise Lost*. But its relations to it are by no means so numerous as those of Du Bartas.

2. See Pritchard, *The Influence of the Fathers upon Milton, with Especial Reference to St. Augustine*, MS. dissertation, Cornell University, 1925; Kathleen E. Hartwell, *Lactantius and Milton*, Cambridge, 1929.

3. Hartwell, the same.

4. Francis Barham, *Adamus Exul of Grotius, or The Prototype of Paradise Lost*, 1839.

as to the matter of philosophical ideas and as to the world of concrete facts. It is therefore suggested that the work of Du Bartas is the only possible work between the Middle Ages and Milton in which survives from the Middle Ages almost the entire body of the basic stuff of *Paradise Lost*, arranged in very much the same form, devoted to much the same grand objectives, and expressed repeatedly in language so similar as to preclude all possibility that these agreements should be denominated in any loose sense mere parallels.[1] So close, indeed, is the language in a multitude of cases as to satisfy anyone of direct relationship, unless he refuses to accept as evidence anything less than slavish copying.

1. Parallels, along with very many other legitimate forms of proof, will of course be offered in evidence where it is natural to offer them. This study does not propose to avoid one of the legitimate types of evidence in order to escape the attack of the parallel baiter of the "parallel chaser," neither group sometimes having read widely enough in Renaissance or Medieval literature to know the difference between a borrowing and a commonplace. MacKerrow, one of the greatest of living bibliographers, has taken the trouble to state the legitimate employment of the parallel passage as one among many kinds of evidence of borrowing in *Review of English Studies*, 1, 362–363. His judgment should control all excessive statements on either side of the question as to the legitimacy of the function of parallels by way of proof of indebtedness.

Chapter II

MEDIEVAL AND RENAISSANCE COMMONPLACES
IN *PARADISE LOST*

NOTE. The references in this study are not to Alexander Grosart's rare and expensive edition of Sylvester's translation (Chertsey Worthies Library) London, 1880, but to the comparatively common and more easily accessible edition, *Du Bartas His Divine Weekes and Workes:* London, 1641. In this edition the lines are not numbered. The citations from Du Bartas I have therefore referred to by page and column as follows: right-hand column, top, centre, bottom, — rt, rc, rb; left-hand column, top, centre, bottom, — lt, lc, lb. The Milton references are to A. W. Verity's edition of *Paradise Lost*, Cambridge University Press, 1921. Milton's capitalization, spelling, and punctuation are in great confusion in the standard editions. I have followed Verity.

THERE will now be given a list of works, which, though by no means exhaustive,[1] is sufficient to show that the thoughts and ideas in *Paradise Lost* which investigators of Milton since 1917 have been attempting to trace to particular sources, are for the most part the common property of Medieval and Renaissance writers. If this conclusion is correct, it logically follows that the occasional appearance of these ideas in individual works, unless phrased in language very similar to Milton's, is insufficient evidence on which to base the claim that Milton was directly influenced. The list of works assembled will serve the additional purpose of showing that, whereas only a few of these ideas occur in the individual authors, practically all of them occur in both Du Bartas and Milton, as the first reference at the begin-

---

1. The list could be extended indefinitely. For example, an examination of books in the British Museum and the Harvard College Library makes it obvious that, under the heading *God* or *The Freedom of the Will*, the bibliography alone would make a book.

ning of each footnote makes clear. It will also help to show how often we, in our modern arrogance, are pleased to term "modernity" what is in reality medievalism.

I. GOD

(1) The Father. His attributes. "Immutable, immortal, infinite." [1] (2) God's *goodness* was the cause of creation. [2] (3) What did God find to do before creation and why was he so *late* in creating? [3] (4) God is invisible. [4] (5) God fills all space — pantheism. [5] (6) The Son of God or the *Word*. Differences between the functions of God the Father and the Word. Did he originate at the same time as God "in time" or "in eternity"? [6] (7) Is the Word

1. Du Bartas, 1 r; *Paradise Lost*, iii, 373; Saurat, *Milton: Man and Thinker*, London, 1925, pp. 122, 113–123; Martin A. Larson, *Milton and Servetus, P.M.L.A.* (1926), XLI, 891 ff.

2. Du Bartas, 2 lc; *P.L.*, vii, 171; Margaret L. Bailey, *Milton and Jakob Boehme*, New York, 1914, p. 147; Plato, Jowett's translation, New York, 1897, II, 30, 31, 34; F. E. Robbins, *The Hexaemeral Literature*, University of Chicago Press, 1912, pp. 4, 5, 30, 38, 53, 73–74 (Robbins cites sixteen writers, beginning with Philo Judaeus, about A.D. 40, and ending with St. Augustine); O. H. Prior, *L'Image du Monde*, Lausanne, 1913, p. 62; Tasso, *Mondo Creato, Argomento*, Giornata Prima, ii, 186, 189.

3. Du Bartas, 2 lc (see marginal gloss, Sylvester); *P.L.*, vii, 92; Robbins, pp. 53, 66 (cites Augustine, Parmenides, Lucretius, Bruno).

4. Du Bartas, 1 rb; *P.L.*, iii, 375; Saurat, pp. 118, 119, 289; Larson, *P.M.L.A.*, XLI, 903, 907.

5. Du Bartas, 1 rb, 154 lc ("not as *all-filling*; God alone is so"), 96 rt; *P.L.*, v, 468 ff.; vii, 168; Saurat, p. 15 and index; Larson, *P.M.L.A.*, XLI, 900, 918 ff.; Bailey, p. 142; Greenlaw, *Spenser's Influence on Paradise Lost, Studies in Philology*, XVII, 340; Harris Fletcher, *Milton's Rabbinical Readings*, University of Illinois Press, 1930, p. 144; Nicolson, *Milton and The Conjectura Cabbalistica, Philological Quarterly*, VI, 11; E. C. Baldwin, *Milton and Plato's Timæus, P.M.L.A.*, XXXV, 216; Robbins, p. 74 (Erigena, Johannus Scotus). God or matter called "this all," Du Bartas, 11, 39, 108 (for the prevalency of the phrase in the Renaissance, see R. V. Merrill, *The Platonism of Du Bellay*, University of Chicago Press, 1925, pp. 24–26).

6. Du Bartas, 2 lc (first engendered by the Father, but not "in time"); *P.L.*, iii, 383; v, 603–604; Greenlaw, *Studies in Philology*, XVII, 337, 345; Saurat, pp. 118, 290; Kathleen E. Hartwell, *Lactantius and Milton*, Harvard University Press, 1929, p. 106; Larson, *P.M.L.A.*, XLI, 924 ff.; Robbins, p. 15 (cites Philo Judaeus and Theophilus of Antioch); Tasso, *M.C.*, i, 93.

equal to God?[1] (8) Did the Son or Word precede the angels in Creation?[2] (9) The Word was the *instrumental*, ministerial side of God in all the creative processes — of the world, the earth, Adam.[3] (10) The Holy Ghost or the Spirit Eternal or Wisdom.[4] (11) "*Impregnating*" function of the Holy Spirit.[5]

II. ANGELS

(1) Created when? Next "in time" or "eternity" to the Word or Son?[6] (2) Free will of angels.[7] (3) Angels identified with the "Heavens," "light," the "stars."[8] (4) Whether angels are in a lesser degree Sons of God.[9] (5) Angels' functions. Messengers.[10]

1. Du Bartas 2 lc; Bailey, pp. 144, 145; Hartwell, p. 98; Tasso, *M.C.*, i, 95, 96.

2. Du Bartas, 2 lc; *P.L.*, iii, 383–384; Bailey, p. 145; Saurat, pp. 274, 290; Hartwell, p. 99; Larson, *P.M.L.A.*, XLI, 907.

3. Du Bartas, 2 lb (the Word is called "the great World's Father"); *P.L.*, vii, 162 ff., 175 ff., 190 ff.; v, 835–837; Bailey, p. 145; Saurat, pp. 119, 120; Greenlaw, *Studies in Philology*, XVII, 337; Hartwell, p. 98; Larson, *P.M.L.A.*, XLI, 907–920; Robbins, pp. 15, 20; Francis Barham, *Adamus Exul of Grotius, or The Prototype of Paradise Lost*, London, 1839, p. 18; *Caedmon's Genesis*, III. 110–111, "opaet theos woruldgesceaft þurh word gewearp woruldcyninges."

4. Du Bartas, 2 lb; *P.L.*, i, 21 ff.; vii, 235 ff.; Saurat, p. 290; Larson, *P.M.L.A.*, XLI, 921 ff.; Fletcher, pp. 109 ff., 115 ff., 121 ff.; Robbins, p. 48.

5. Du Bartas, 4 lc; *P.L.*, i, 21; vii, 235, 236; Bailey, pp. 144–146; Saurat, p. 135; Nicolson, *Philological Quarterly*, VI, 12; Larson, *P.M.L.A.*, XLI, 930; Fletcher, pp. 90, 118, 123, 124, 126, 127, 130, 143, 148; Grotius (Barham), p. 18; Robbins, p. 39 (cites Basil, A.D. 379, Jerome, Ambrose, Augustine, Abelard, and ten others, Du Bartas and Milton among them, with reference even to the bird sitting on the eggs), p. 48.

6. Du Bartas, 6 lc; *P.L.*, iii, 383–391; v, 603–604, De Doctrina, IV, 84; Greenlaw, *Studies in Philology*, XVII, 337; Saurat, p. 274; Robbins, pp. 45, 61 (Serverianus, Theodorus, Milton); Tasso, *M.C.*, Giornata Seconda.

7. Du Bartas, 6 lc; *P.L.*, iii, 100; v, 525–543; Saurat, pp. 129, 270; Nicolson, *The Spirit World of Milton and More*, Studies in Philology, XXII, 447; O. F. Prior, *L'Image du Monde*, p. 64 (says man is superior to angels because they had not free will).

8. Du Bartas, 6 lc; *P.L.*, iii, 390; v, 160, 161, 600; Bailey, p. 147; Robbins, pp. 21, 68 (St. Augustine), 78, 79 (Bede, Neckam, and others); *L'Image du Monde*, p. 91; Tasso, *M. C.*, Giornata Prima, ll. 495–503 (*al primo lume, I secondi splendori, Angeli santi*).

9. Du Bartas, 6; *P.L.*, v, 447, 863; xi, 80, 84; Greenlaw, *Studies in Philology*, XVII, 353; Saurat, pp. 117, 253, 257, 258; Larson, *P.M.L.A.*, XLI, 907, 909, 931.

10. Du Bartas, 7 lc; 154 lc; Greenlaw, *Studies in Philology*, XVII, 345–346 (footnote); Nicolson, the same, XXII, 449.

Nature works on matter.[1]   (5) Matter essentially *good*.[2]   (6) "Light" first of things created by the Word or Son.[3]   (7) Not identical with the Sun.[4]   (8) *"Earth self-balanced* on its centre hung."[5]

VIII. Evil

(1) God did not create evil.[6] (2) *Permissive* theory of evil. God allows it.[7] (3) *Free will.*[8] (4) Did God condemn the Serpent or Satan inside of Serpent mysteriously interpreted?[9]

xxxv, 216; Nicolson, *Philological Quarterly*, vi, 11; Larson, p. 902; Robbins, p. 74 (Erigena, Johannes Scotus). Saurat, p. 279, says this makes Milton "modern."

1. Du Bartas, 3 rb; *P.L.*, ii, 1037, iii, 455, viii, 26; Nicolson, *Milton and Hobbes*, *Studies in Philology*, xxiii, 420, 421 ff.; *L'Image du Monde*, pp. 86 ff.

2. *P.L.*, v, 468 ff.; Saurat, pp. 137, 279 (Saurat says, p. 279, "This makes Milton a *modern* man"); Fletcher, p. 144; Nicolson, *Studies in Philology*, xxiii, 413; *Philological Quarterly*, vi, 13; Baldwin, *P.M.L.A.*, xxxv, 216; Larson, *P.M.L.A.*, xli, 902.

3. Du Bartas, 5 rc; *P.L.*, vii, 244; iii, 1; Saurat, pp. 316, 317; Robbins, p. 46.

4. Du Bartas, 5 r; *P.L.*, vii, 247–248; iii, 8; Saurat, pp. 316, 317; Fletcher, p. 149; Robbins, pp. 46 (cites Basil and others), 49, 51 (cites Milton, 80, footnote, Du Bartas, Milton); Tasso, *M.C.*, Giornata Quarta.

5. Du Bartas, 25 lb; *P.L.*, ii, 1052; viii, 17; Du Bartas, 25 lt, 60 lc; *P.L.*, vii, 242 (smaller than smallest star); Fletcher, pp. 136, 137; Shakespeare, *King John*, "the earth which of itself is peised well"; Robbins, p. 48 (Basil).

6. Du Bartas, 115 r; 93 lt; *P.L.*, iii, 97; Robbins, p. 5.

7. Du Bartas, 7 lc; *P.L.*, i, 212; vii, 237; Saurat, pp. 127, 130, 277, 293; Nicolson, *Studies in Philology*, xxiii, 432.

8. Du Bartas, 93; *P.L.*, iii, 96 ff.; Saurat, pp. 128, 129, 271; Larson, *P.M.L.A.*, xli, 915; Greenlaw, *Studies in Philology*, xiv, 213; Nicolson, *Studies in Philology*, xxii, 452; *Studies in Philology*, xxiii, 418, 428, 429, 431, 432; J. P. Pritchard, *The Influence of the Fathers on Milton with Especial Reference to St. Augustine*, MS. dissertation, Cornell University, 1925, pp. 68 ff.; *L'Image du Monde*, pp. 64 ff.; Grotius (Barham), pp. 35, 41. See further below, pp. 48, 69 ff.

9. Du Bartas, 90 rc, 91 lc; *P.L.*, ix, 413; x, 84, 173–174 (apparently a contradiction); Saurat, pp. 250, 261; Nicolson, *Philological Quarterly*, vi, 16; Fletcher, pp. 199, 200; Grotius (Barham), pp. 14, 34.

IX. ADAM. MAN

(1) Meaning of *"in the image of God"*; a physical or mental likeness?[1] (2) Emphasis on *Reason* in man as governing faculty.[2] (3) Chaos in man (microcosmos) without Reason, as in cosmos without reasoning God.[3] (4) Eve less Reason than Adam.[4] (5) Adam stands *upright*.[5] (6) Adam's mental and physical perfection before the Fall.[6]

1. Du Bartas, 53 lb, 53 rc, 57 lc, 83 rc; *P.L.*, iv, 291–292; vii, 527–528; xi, 515–525; Baldwin, *P.M.L.A.*, xxxv, 211; Nicolson, *Studies in Philology*, xxII, 437; *Philological Quarterly*, vI, 13, 14; Robbins, pp. 32, 33, 59 (Basil and his followers; Raleigh's *History of the World*, I, 2, 1; 70; St. Augustine); *L'Image du Monde*, pp. 62 f.; Grotius (Barham), pp. 16, 17, 39.

2. Du Bartas, 53 rc, 83 rc; *P.L.*, v, 487; vii, 508; ix, 124–128; Greenlaw, *Studies in Philology*, xIV, 214; Saurat, pp. 170, 171, 275; Hartwell, pp. 75, 77; Baldwin, *P.M.L.A.*, xxxv, 212; Nicolson, *Philological Quarterly*, vI, 9; *Studies in Philology*, xxIII, 418, 419 ff.; Robbins, pp. 32, 33 (cites Origen, St. Augustine, and others); Grotius (Barham), p. 16.

3. Du Bartas, 52 rb, 53 rc; Nicolson, *Studies in Philology*, xxIII, 429, 431 ff.

4. Du Bartas, 53 rt; *P.L.*, iv, 300; Nicolson, *Philological Quarterly*, vI, 15.

5. Du Bartas, 53 rc; *P.L.*, vii, 508, 509; xi, 9; Hartwell, p. 75; Robbins, pp. 10, 56, 71 (St. Augustine).

6. Du Bartas, 53 rc, 55 rt, 83 rc; *P.L.*, iv, 291 ff.; v, 487 ff.; vii, 505; viii, 219–223; Nicolson, *Philological Quarterly*, vi, 8, 9; Fletcher, pp. 187–192; Robbins, p. 33 (Philo Judaeus); *L'Image du Monde*, p. 180 ("souverains de beaute et de sens et de force"); Tasso, *M.C.*, Giornata Sesta, Argomenta.

X. Effects of the Fall of Adam[1] on Adam and Eve

(1) Entrance of passions (lust, hate, and others) into microcosmos.[2] (2) Diseases.[3] (3) Animals attack man and herbs become harmful.[4] (4) Effect on the "change of seasons" and stars.[5]

XI. Souls[6]

(1) Propagated with body; not separate from body.[7] (2) Animals have souls.[8] (3) Soul can leave the body and ascend by four stages to Heaven.[9]

XII. Scheme of Salvation of Man

How man may attain to a state preferable even to the original state of innocence of Adam. Main justification.[10]

1. Du Bartas, 96 ff. (*The Furies*); *P.L.*, ix, 782, 1000; xi, 182 ff.; Greenlaw, *Studies in Philology*, xvii, 326; Saurat, pp. 145, 150, 152, 170, 171, 275; Fletcher, pp. 192–207; Nicolson, *Philological Quarterly*, vi, 17; George Edmundson, *Milton and Vondel*, London, 1885 (*Lucifer*, iv, 1502–1508); *L'Image du Monde*, pp. 156, 180, 181; Robbins, p. 70 (St. Augustine); Pritchard, pp. 68 ff.

2. Du Bartas, 96 rt, 98 lt; *P.L.*, ix, 1123 ff.; Saurat, pp. 146, 150; Fletcher, pp. 206 ff; Agar, *Milton and Plato*, p. 13.

3. Du Bartas, 98 r ff.; *P.L.*, xi, 473–490.

4. Du Bartas, 96 lb; *P.L.*, iv, 341 ff., 256; xi, 182 ff.; Robbins, pp. 5, 38, 70 (eighteen references beginning with Theophilus of Alexandrea A.D. *ca.* 168), 51 (lists of animals and plants: Basil, Ambrose, Glyca, Pisides, Du Bartas), 59 (Pisides).

5. Du Bartas, 93 lb, 96 lc, rc ff.; *P.L.*, ix, 782 ff.; x, 212 ff., 669 ff., 1063; Bailey, p. 133; Greenlaw, *Studies in Philology*, xvii, 326, 354; Saurat, pp. 145 ff.; O. Kuhns, *Dante's Influence on Milton*, *Modern Language Notes*, xiii, 7; *L'Image du Monde*, p. 156.

6. Du Bartas, 55 r, 56 l; *P.L.*, vii, 387 ff.; Saurat, pp. 141 ff.; Nicolson, *Studies in Philology*, xxii, 433 ff.; Agar, p. 11; Merrill, pp. 71–75; Tasso, *M.C.*, Giornata Sesta; Robbins, pp. 10, 32, 57.

7. Du Bartas, 55 rb; Du Bartas says, *separate*, p. 4 rb; *P.L.*, vii, 387 ff.; Saurat, pp. 141, 142, 313, 318; Baldwin, *P.M.L.A.*, xxxv, 211; Robbins, p. 57.

8. *P.L.*, vii, 387 ff.; St. Augustine, *De Civitate Dei*, xiii, 24; Saurat, pp. 141, 277; Tasso, *M.C.*, Giornata Sesta (man's soul differs from animal's soul); Robbins, p. 32, note 3 (Philo Judaeus).

9. Du Bartas, 56 lc; Greenlaw, *Studies in Philology*, xiv, 207; xvii, 348–356; Robbins, p. 10 (cites Philo Judaeus, Ambrose, Pisides and others, leading to Du Bartas).

10. Du Bartas, 93 rc; *P.L.*, xi, 23 ff.; xii, 464, 586, 587; Saurat, pp. 131, 175, 253, 277,

XIII. THEORY OF KNOWLEDGE

(1) Distrust of over-curious inquiry into secrets or mysteries of God.[1] (2) Learn to know of God through the *Book of God's Works*.[2] (3) Book of God's works refutes atheism.[3] (4) Book of God's works compels our wonder and admiration.[4]

292, 297; Greenlaw, *Studies in Philology*, xvii, 325; Nicolson, *Philological Quarterly*, vi, 18; Fletcher, p. 204.

1. Du Bartas, 2 rc, 17 rb (gloss) 18 rt; *P.L.*, vii, 95; viii, 70 ff., 74 ff., 119 ff., 184 ff.; Edmundson, *Milton and Vondel*, p. 59 (quoting *Lucifer*, ii, 555–558); Greenlaw, *Studies in Philology*, xiv, 211; xvii, 325, 328; Saurat, p. 297; Kuhns, *Modern Language Notes*, xiii, 6 (*Par.* xxix, 85 ff.); Hartwell, pp. 90–92; *L'Image du Monde*, p. 70; Tasso, *M.C.*, Giornata Sesta; Robbins, p. 69; Pritchard, p. 72.

2. Du Bartas, 2 rc, 2 rb, 3 lt; *P.L.*, iii, 46 ff., 695, 696; viii, 66–69; xi, 327 ff.; Greenlaw, *Studies in Philology*, xvii, 330, 348, 349, 351; Gilbert, *Milton and Galileo, Studies in Philology*, xix, 170; Bacon, *Advancement of Learning* (ed. Wright), pp. 8, 10; *L'Image du Monde*, pp. 70, 72; Tasso, *M.C.*, Giornata Quarta; Edmundson, p. 57 (quoting *Lucifer*, ii, 483–491).

3. Du Bartas, 2 lt (purpose of Sepmaine), 116 (sixteen points against atheism); Nicolson, *Studies in Philology*, xxiii, 405 ff.; Bacon, *Of Atheism* ("God's ordinary works refute It").

4. Du Bartas (greater part of first seven books of *Divine Weekes*), 2 rb, 3 lt, 49 lt, 53 lt; *P.L.*, viii, 75 ff. (see further, pp. 82–85 below); Nicolson, *Studies in Philology*, xxiii, 421; Robbins, pp. 28, 77; *L'Image du Monde*, pp. 70, 71; Barham, p. 18.

Chapter III

COMPARISON OF DU BARTAS AS SOURCE OF MILTON WITH OTHER SOURCES RECENTLY SUGGESTED [1]

I HAVE attempted in Chapter II to show that recent investigation of Milton has in the main been concerned with currents and systems of thought in *Paradise Lost* which had become during the Middle Ages and Renaissance the commonplaces of a variety of literary types. It has also appeared that the blocks of literary material, as well as the philosophical approaches to this material, which occur in relatively small units in the authors hitherto examined, occur almost in their entirety in Du Bartas, a poet with whom Milton was certainly familiar. The next step in the proof that the most neglected of the sources of Milton is the most important of all will make it clear that the expression of these ideas, themes, and blocks of material is in the main, either individually or collectively or according to arrangement and structure, much closer to Milton in Du Bartas than in the other writers. Often, indeed, the parallels are so close as to leave no doubt as to direct relationship. That Milton was indebted to many of the writers cited there can be no doubt. No one can examine carefully Greenlaw's study of Spenser and Milton, Miss Nicolson's study of Henry More and Milton, Fletcher's discussion of Milton's rabbinical reading, Miss Hartwell's *Lactantius and Milton*, and the work of Saurat and the many other scholars mentioned in Chapter II, without concluding that Milton in some

---

[1] Italics in all quotations from this point on are generally mine.

cases certainly, and in other cases possibly, had first-hand familiarity with the writings investigated. But I maintain that none of the works brought forward to explain the appearance of these materials in *Paradise Lost* or the form which they finally assume there is of more importance in these regards than the *Divine Weekes and Workes* of Sylvester, and that in no other single instance is the indebtedness of Milton so extensive. With this in mind, let us examine several of these studies.

Greenlaw

Modern scholarship owes much to Greenlaw. Two of his articles assisted in launching that movement in Milton research which has resulted in revealing to thinking readers a philosophical Milton. His two studies, appearing in 1917 and 1920,[1] made clear the substantial indebtedness of Milton to Spenser both in the philosophic and idealistic content of *Paradise Lost* and in its literary form. Before accepting his conclusions, however, we must investigate Du Bartas with the same particularity with which he investigated Spenser. Greenlaw recognizes, as others have done, the *general* significance of Du Bartas: "From Spenser," he says, "we turn to a French poet . . . whose influence on Spenser and Milton was very marked." [2] In both of his articles, however, the traditional view of Du Bartas as related to Milton is perpetuated. Greenlaw always discounts the directness of his influence. He concedes in no single instance a direct borrowing by Milton from this source, even in those cases in which Du Bartas, as will be shown, has preceded Spenser in developing the same theme. In his first study he does not mention Du Bartas. In his second

1. *A Better Teacher Than Aquinas, Studies in Philology*, xiv (1917), 196–217; *Spenser's Influence on Paradise Lost, Studies in Philology*, xvii (1920), 320–359.
2. *The New Science and English Literature in the Seventeenth Century, The Johns Hopkins Alumni Magazine*, xiii (1925), 353 ff.

study, *Spenser's Influence on Paradise Lost*, Du Bartas, when referred to at all, is not called a source, but a "supposed source": "the mysteries, for example, in Du Bartas, in . . . the supposed sources." [1] The mysteries, indeed, as already suggested, are not even a supposed source but interesting analogues.

Unlike Greenlaw's second study, which presents specific evidence of Milton's debt to Spenser, his first study, *A Better Teacher Than Aquinas*, is "based not on the presence of verbal imitations or parallels in incident but on Milton's own testimony of his debt, on his clear statements in *Areopagitica*, and on the philosophical affinity of the two poems." [2] There are, nevertheless, even in this first study, important conclusions which cannot be accepted without reckoning with Du Bartas far more carefully than he has as yet been reckoned with. For example, Greenlaw remarks, "In thus fusing the Christian dogma with a philosophy ultimately Platonic Milton is a child of the Renaissance. In making epic the means of such fusion he is both a child of the Renaissance and the poetical son of Spenser." [3] Now Du Bartas as the culmin-

---

1. *Studies in Philology*, XVII, 325.   2. The same, XIV, 212.

3. The same, XIV, 212. Miss Nicolson (*Studies in Philology*, XXII, 451) calls attention to the fact that More's "universe is as completely ordered and planned in the mind of God as is Milton's" — "a neo-Platonic idea which Milton suggests when he says (V, 571):

> 'What surmounts the reach
> Of human sense I shall delineate so,
> By likening spiritual to corporal forms,
> As may express them best, though what if Earth
> Be but the shadow of Heaven, and things therein
> Each to other like, more than on Earth is thought?'"

Larson (*P.M.L.A.*, XLI, 904) quotes Milton:

> How good, how fair,
> Answering his great idea,

with the remark, "Notice the Platonic conception. We need not pause further to remark upon the identity of the creative theories held by Servetus and Milton." Fletcher (*Milton's Rabbinical Readings*, pp. 114 ff.) devotes several pages to Ben Gerson's *Understanding and Her Relation to the Plan of Creation*, suggesting that "it was perhaps the origin of Milton's plan."

ating point in the development of the Hexaemeral motives in the Renaissance epic is an extraordinarily fine example of just this "fusing Christian dogma with a philosophy ultimately Platonic." Exactly this fusion had in fact been going on from Philo (A.D. 40) to St. Augustine and later. Milton's use of the Platonism of Du Bartas will be fully treated in Chapter IV. Here, however, we must note in passing how close is Milton to Du Bartas in the entire matter of creation, especially as to "fusing Christian dogma with a philosophy ultimately Platonic." Thus Du Bartas says, as he begins his account of creation:

> It may be also, that he meditated
> *The World's Idea*, ere it was created.   DB, 2 lc

Milton says, immediately after describing the creation:

> Thence to behold this new-created *World*
> The addition of his empire — how it showed
> In prospect from his throne, how good, how fair,
> *Answering his great Idea*.   vii, 554 ff.

Du Bartas has:

>   Th' All-working Word alone
> Made Nothing be *All's womb and Embryon*,
> Th' eternall Plot, *th' Idea fore-conceiv'd*,
> The wondrous Form of all that Form receiv'd,
> Did in the Work-man's spirit divinely lie;
> And, yer it was, the World was wondrously.   DB, 140 rb

Milton condenses thus:

> Th' Earth was formed, but, in the *womb* as yet
> Of waters, *embryon*, immature, involved,
> Appeared not.   vii, 276 ff.

Greenlaw notes that Spenser "in the Second Hymne" speaks of the "paterne" used by the great "Work maister." [1] Du Bartas, however, is distinctly in point here:

---

1. *Studies in Philology*, XVII, 337, note.

> Th' Eternall Trine-One, spreading even the Tent
> Of th' All enlightning glorious Firmament,
> *Fill'd it with figures*; and in various Marks
> There pourtray'd Tables of his future Works.
> See here the *pattern* of a silver Brook.   DB, 141 lt

Milton's God

> . . . Took the golden compasses, prepared
> In God's *eternal store*, to circumscribe
> This Universe.   vii, 225 ff.

The extraordinary details in which Milton is similar to Du Bartas in carrying out the "plan preconceived" in God's mind must, however, be reserved for the next chapter.[1]

The second extremely important conclusion reached by Greenlaw in his first study of Spenser and Milton is the similarity in the two of "the control of all powers, mental desires as well as physical desires, by the rational element in the soul. This, once more, is followed by Milton."[2] Greenlaw adds in a footnote,[3] "The most convincing proof of Milton's indebtedness to Spenser's Platonism in this respect is supplied by the explanation of Eve's dream by Adam in v, 100 ff. Adam says that in the soul are many lesser *faculties that serve Reason as chief*; among them is Fancy, whose office is to form imaginations of all external things supplied by the five senses. These imaginations are to be tested by Reason, framing our knowledge or opinion. So Spenser describes the house of Alma (II, ix. 10 ff.)." Place the Du Bartas passage on dreams beside Milton's and notice the curious manner in which it has contributed to the wonderful explanation of dreams in *Paradise Lost*:

---

1. Pp. 91 ff.
2. *Studies in Philology*, xiv, 211. Miss Nicolson also calls attention to this in Milton, *Studies in Philology*, xxiii, 418; see p. 21, note 6, above.
3. *Studies in Philology*, xiv, 212.

But know that in the *soul*
Are many lesser *faculties* that serve
Reason as *chief*; among these *Fancy* next
Her office holds; of all external things,
Which the five watchful senses repre-
  sent,
She forms imaginations, aery shapes,
Which Reason joining or disjoining,
  frames
All what we affirm or what deny, and
  call
Our knowledge or opinion . . .

. . . .

Oft in her absence mimic Fansy wakes
To imitate her; but, misjoining shapes
Wild work produces oft, and most in
  dreams.   v, 100 ff.

Sometimes by you, O you all-faining
  Dreams,
We gain this good; but not when Bac-
  chus streams
And glutton vapours over-flow the
  Brain,

. . . .

Nor when the *Spirit* of *lies*, our spirit
  deceives,
And guilefull visions in our *fancy*
  leaves:

. . . .

But *when no more the soules chiefe
  faculties*,
Are 'sperst to serve the body many
  wayes.   DB, 84 rc

In his second study, *Spenser's Influence on Paradise Lost,* Green-law varies his method of proof and offers quotations from Spenser bearing directly on quotations from Milton. It is possible, says Greenlaw, "to be even more specific in regard to the direct influence of Spenser on Milton in both incident and the very structure of *Paradise Lost* itself," [1] adding "but the end of the study is not to add to the bewildering number of analogues of this great poem." In practically every instance, however, in which Spenser is cited, a Du Bartas passage may account for both Spenser and Milton.

Chapter IV will give in detail each Du Bartas borrowing in every book of *Paradise Lost*; but some of the more noticeably convincing parallels may here be cited in passing. Greenlaw says: [2]

Merely to name the chief passages in *Paradise Lost* in which this theme of Nature is treated is to become conscious of how great a place it held in Milton's thought. In the first place, there is his *constant interest in the origin of the universe.* His story of the Creation, *expanded as it is from the account in Genesis,* is

---

1. *Studies in Philology,* XVII, 321 ff.
2. The same, XVII, 325 ff.

similar to what we find elsewhere — in the mysteries, for example, in Du Bartas, in certain of the supposed sources. But this feature of the poem does not give any adequate idea of the way in which the *problem of origins interested him*. The constant use of the *old physics*, — the realm of Chaos and Night, *the war of the elements*, the description of Hell as a universe of death where Nature, perverse, breeds monstrous things; *his account of the abyss, the womb of Nature and perhaps her grave*, are a few of many examples that might be cited. His interest is physical, not biological. The Garden of Adonis, an ancient account of the origin of species developed by Spenser in one of the purple passages of *The Faerie Queene*, he refers to as "mystic," showing that he understood Spenser's use and development of the myth, but he does not go into detail; for him the origin of life is the origin described in Genesis. But everywhere he is interested in the *physical*. The prayer of Adam and Eve to the God who is in Nature (V. 153 ff.) is of this character. So also is his description of the changes that took place *after the Fall of Man — the seasons, the zones, the phases of the moon, the winds, and, above all, the inimical power of Nature, her hostility to Man*:

> Thus began
> Outrage from lifeless things.

Du Bartas needs to be considered in connection with every point thus emphasized by Greenlaw:

For *Hot, Cold, Moist, Dry* four champions fierce,
Strive here for mastery, and *to battle bring*
Their embryon atoms; they around the flag
Of *each his faction*, in their several *clans*,
Light-armed or heavy, sharp, smooth, swift, or slow
Swarm populous, unnumbered.
                ii, 898 ff.

Where all difference lackt:
Where th' Elements lay jumbled all together,
Where *hot* and *cold* were jarring each with either;
The blunt with sharp, the *dank* against the *drie*;
The hard with soft . . .

and while this *brawl* did last.
                DB, 3rt

for (still opposite)
With *tooth* and *nail* as deadly *foes they fight*.   DB, 11 lt

Earth, Aire, and Fire, were with Water mixt;

As yet this world was not, and *Chaos* wild

Where in *confusion reigned such debate:* . . .

Reigned where these Heavens now roll.   v, 577–578

This was not then the World:
'twas but the Matter,
The Nurcery whence it should issue after;
Or rather, *the Embryon that . . .*
Was to be born.   DB, 3rb

Till at *his second bidding* Darkness fled,
Light shon, and order from disorder sprung,
Swift *to their several quarters hasted then*
The cumbrous elements — earth, flood, air, fire;
And this *ethereal quintessence* of Heaven
Flew upward, spirited with various forms,
That rolled orbicular, and *turned* to *stars.*   iii, 712 ff.

The Lord high-Marshal, *unto each his quarter*
Had not assigned . . .   DB, 3rc

When the Mouth Divine
Op'ned, to each his proper place t' assign,
Fire flew to Fire, Water to Water slid,
Aire clung to Aire, and Earth with *Earth* abid.
Earth, as the Lees, and heavy drosse of All
(After his kinde) *did to the bottome fall.*

the . . . nimble Fire [stars]
Did *. . . aspire*

Unto the top . . .
. . . mounted in sparks [stars]
                    DB, 11 rb

Darkness profound
Covered the *Abyss*; but on the watery calm
His *brooding wings* the *Spirit of God* outspread,

Darkness . . .
Muffled the face of that *profound Abyss . . .*
So did *God's Spirit* delight itselfe a space
To move itselfe upon the floting Masse
.   .   .   .   .   .

And vital virtue infused, and vital warmth,
Throughout the fluid mass, but *downward purged*
The black, tartareous, cold, *infernal dregs,*
Adverse to life; then founded, then conglobed,

Or as a Hen that fain would hatch a *Brood*
.   .   .   .   .   .
Sits close thereon, and with her lively heat, . . .
Even in such sort seemed the *Spirit Eternall*
. . . To *brood* upon this Gulf . . .

Like things to like, the rest to several place
Disparted.   vii, 233 ff.

Quickening the parts, inspiring power in each,
From so *foule Lees*, so faire a World to fetch   DB, 4 lt

This wilde Abyss,
The womb of Nature, and perhaps her grave.   ii, 910–911

This *world* to *Chaos* shall again *return*.
                                        DB, 226 lt

Greenlaw continues to quote similar material treated similarly in Spenser and Milton: "The theory of Chaos and Night, of the abyss, whence came the World." . . . "This material is found in many places in Spenser's poetry, and is very similar to the theory used by Milton." [1] Passages are then quoted from Spenser which illustrate the similarity of his ideas to Milton's as to the origins of the universe and the origins of life on the earth. The following passages from Du Bartas may be suggested as the origin of both the Milton and Spenser passages mentioned by Greenlaw: [2]

The first *seminary*
Of all things that are borne to live and dye,
According to their kynds.
          The Faerie Queene, iii, 6, 30

This was not then the World: 'twas but the Matter,
The *Nurcery* whence it should issue after;
Or rather, the *Embryon*, that within a Weeke
Was to be born; for that huge lump was like
The shape-less burthen in the Mother's *womb*   DB, 3 rb

An huge eternal chaos, which supplyes
The substances of Natures fruitfull progenyes.
          The Faerie Queene, iii, 6, 36

The seedes, of which all things at first were bred,
Shall in *great Chaos wombe* againe be hid   *The Ruines of Rome*, xxii [3]

I means that *Chaos*, that self-jarring Mass,
          .   .   .   .   .   .
Was the rich Matter and *Matrix*, whence
The Heav'ns should issue, and the Elements.   DB, 10 lt

---

1. *Studies in Philology*, xvii, 331.
2. Spenser of course read Du Bartas in the original.
3. Translation of Du Bellay.

For Spenser's idea: "*Venus* represents *form* or spirit: *Adonis* represents *matter*": [1]

> eterne in mutabilitie,
> And by *succession* made *perpetuall*,
> Transformed oft, and chaunged diverslie;
> For him the Father of all *formes* they call.
>
> *The Faerie Queene*, iii, 6, 47

there is Du Bartas:

> Here's nothing constant: nothing still doth stay;
> For Birth and Death have still *successive sway*.
> Here *one thing springs not till another die:*
> Onely *the Matter lives immortally*.
>
> . . . .
>
> *Change-lesse in Essence: changeable in face,*
> Or like a *Lais*, whose inconstant Love
> Doth every day a thousand times remove;
>
> . . . .
>
> And the new pleasure of her wanton Fire
> Stirs in her still another new Desire:
> Because the *Matter, wounded* deep in Heart
> With various *Love* . . .
> . . . by *successions,*
> *Form after Form receives.*   DB, 11 lb

For Spenser's "infinite shapes" of other living creatures, including "uncouth formes which none yet ever knew," [2] there are, in the Du Bartas Garden of Eden,

> True Beasts, fast in the ground still sticking,
> Feeding on grass, and th' Airy moysture licking.   DB, 86 lt

and many another uncouth form. Greenlaw's statement [3] "that God, the Son and the Angels antedated the earth and man" in Spenser, is applicable to Du Bartas:

> It may be also, that he meditated
> The World's Idea, ere it was created:
> Alone he lived not; for his Son and Spirit
> Were with him aye.   DB, 2 lc

---

1. *Studies in Philology*, xvii, 332.
2. *The Faerie Queene*, iii, 6, 35; *Studies in Philology*, the same.
3. *Studies in Philology*, xvii, 337.

> Whether, This-Day, God made you Angels, bright
> Under the name of Heav'n or of the light

. . . .

> Or whether you [angels] derive your high Descent
> Long time before the World and Firmament.   DB, 6 lc

Greenlaw refers also to Milton's description of the changes that took place after the Fall of Man as the result of Sin — "the seasons, the zones, the phases of the moon, the winds and, above all, the inimical power of Nature, her hostility to Man":[1]

> Thus began
> Outrage from lifeless things.   x, 706–707

This exact scheme is so elaborately worked out by Du Bartas in an entire section of his work (*The Furies*), and Milton follows the scheme so carefully, not only in regard to the matters mentioned before but also in regard to the rise of the passions and the coming of diseases, that, as will be shown in detail in connection with Books x, xi, and xii of *Paradise Lost*, it is very probable that Milton was in this point following. Du Bartas, although the scheme itself is well known to the Middle Ages.[2] Greenlaw quotes from Spenser's *Hymnes* those passages descriptive of the four stages through which the disembodied Soul passes finally to the presence of God, relating it to Milton,[3] and remarks finally, "This is, of course, the mystic vision or perfect contemplation that is the final state of the Soul's development." Side by side with this material from Spenser — as a possible source[4] both of Spenser and of Milton — I arrange the following extracts from Du Bartas:

1. *Studies in Philology*, xvii, 326.
2. See p. 22, notes 1, 2, 3, 4, above.
3. *Studies in Philology*, xvii, 348, 349, 350, 356.
4. This is to be found, however, in Philo Judaeus, A.D. *ca.* 40. See Robbins, p. 10, and also p. 22, note 9, above.

Spenser	Du Bartas
And let thy soule, whose sins his sorrows wrought,	But above all, that's the divinest Trance
Melt into teares, and grone in grieved thought,	When the Soul's eye beholds God's counternance,
. . . .	. . . .
Then shalt thou feele thy spirit so possest,	And in our face his drad-sweet face he seales;
And ravisht with devouring great desire	. . . .
Of his deare selfe, that shall thy feeble breast	O sacred sight! *sweet rape!* loves soverain bliss!
Inflame with love, and set thee all on fire	Which very loves deer lips dost make us kiss:
With burning zeale, through every part entire,	. . . . . .
That in no earthly thing thou shalt delight,	Which for a time doth Heav'n, with earth contract:
But in his sweet and amiable sight.	Fire that in Limbeck of pure thoughts divine
. . . . . .	Dost purge our thought, and our dull earth refine:
	And mounting us to Heav'n, . . .
	Man (in a trice) in God doost quintessence DB, 84 rb and 85 lt
Then shall thy ravisht soule inspired bee	And though our Soule live as imprison'd here
With heavenly thoughts farre above humane skil,	In our frail Flesh . . .
And thy bright radiant eyes shall plainely see	. . . sometimes, leaving these base slimy heaps,
Th' Idee of his pure glorie present still	. . . above the Clouds she leaps,
Before thy face, that all thy spirits shall fill	Glides through the Aire, and there she learns to know
With *sweete enragement* of celestiall love,	Th' originals of Winde, and Hail, and Snow,
Kindled through sight of those faire things above.	. . . . . .
Heavenly Love, 251 ff.	By th' Aires steep-stairs, she boldly climbs aloft
And, *last, that mightie shining* christall *wall*	To the World's Chambers; Heav'n she visits oft,
Where with he hath encompassed them All.	Stage after Stage: she marketh all the Sphears.
. . . . . .	. . . . . .

For farre above these heavens, which
   here we see,
Be others farre exceeding these in light,
Not bounded, not corrupt, as these
   same bee,
But infinite in largenesse and in hight,
Unmoving, uncorrupt, and spotlesse
   bright,
That need no Sunne t' illuminate their
   spheres,
But their owne native light farre
   passing theirs.
           Heavenly Beautie, 41 ff.

The meanes, therefore, which unto us
   is lent
Him to behold, is on his workes to
   looke,
Which he hath made in beauty excel-
   lent.   *Heavenly Beautie,* 127 ff.

Sweete contentment, that it doth
   bereave
Their soule of sense, through infinite
   delight,
And them transport from flesh into the
   spright.
In which they see such admirable
   things,
As carries them into an extasy,
And heare such heavenly notes and
   carolings,
Of Gods high praise, that filles the
   brasen sky.
          Heavenly Beautie, 257 ff.

She counts their Stars, . . .
. . . and, as if she found
No subject fair enough in all this
   Round
She mounts above the World's ex-
   tremest *Wall,*
Far, far beyond all things corporeall:
Where she beholds her Maker, face to
   face.   56 lc

Or till my selfe (this sinfull robe
   bereav'n,
This rebell Flesh, whose counterpoise
   oppresses
My pilgrim Soule, and ever it de-
   presses)
Shall see the Beauties of that Blessed
   Place:
If (then) I ought shall see, save God's
   bright Face.   17 rb

In these passages from Du Bartas are to be found the main
points in regard to the exact stages of the soul in its progress upward to God to which Greenlaw calls attention. "Man rises," says
Greenlaw, "to these spiritual heights by two means: the contemplation of God, divine dealings with man, and God's revelation of

himself in his created universe." [1] This revelation is, of course, tremendously stressed by Du Bartas, more it would seem than by any other poet of the Renaissance, and is considered at length in its relation to Milton in Chapter V. Here, however, it should be noticed how extraordinarily close Du Bartas is to the following passage quoted by Greenlaw [2] in this connection from Spenser as contributing to Milton:

The meanes, therefore, which unto us is lent Him to behold, is on his *workes to looke*, *Which he has made in beauty* excellent. *Heavenly Love*, 129 ff.	I love *to look on God; but, in this Robe* Of *his great Works, this Universall Globe* . . . . . . God, of himself, incapable to sense, *In's Works reveals him t' our* intelligence. DB, 2 rc

And Du Bartas, more even than Milton or Spenser, emphasizes this approach to God, assigning it as his chief motive for writing his entire Work rather than, as is often said, to confute the Copernican theory:

> And, God the better to behold, behold
> Th' Orb from his Birth.   DB, 3 lc

In the light of these facts, therefore, and of those to be presented in the next chapter, it is impossible to accept as final Greenlaw's statement as to the relative debt of Milton to Spenser and Du Bartas. "It has also shown," he says in reference to his study, "in both cases a comparatively complete system, containing in the works of the two poets, substantially the same elements. Moreover Spenser used these elements to an extent not found in the poets usually cited as Milton's predecessors except Du Bartas; the use of them is wholly different from that of Du Bartas; and it is cognate in every important respect with that of Milton." [3]

1. *Studies in Philology*, xvii, 349.
2. The same, xvii, 350.
3. The same, xvii, 341.

SAURAT

This book does not propose to examine every idea in Du Bartas similar to those ideas collected by Saurat out of works suggested by him as sources of Milton. By referring to Chapter II,[1] the reader will, however, see that in almost every case in which Saurat's work is cited a Du Bartas citation begins the bibliographical note. Some of the more important passages in *Paradise Lost* which Saurat considers in connection with works he is attempting to relate to Milton as bearing upon his modernity, can easily be shown to be directly related to that poet of the French Renaissance whom France would perhaps class as a Medieval pietist.

For example, it is possible with the aid of Du Bartas to show that Saurat's interpretation of those six lines from Milton which he has singled out specifically as "the most important passage in *Paradise Lost* from the philosophical point of view as well as the most characteristic," [2] cannot be accepted. "Here Milton," he continues, "expresses his most striking and, as it seems, his most original idea, from which is derived his conception of matter; since matter is that 'space not vacuous' even after the contraction of God, that which remains of God's powers in space when God has withdrawn his will. It can therefore be asserted that Milton has derived from the *Zohar* his philosophical system. Pantheism, materialism, doctrines of free-will and of fate as God's will — by a truly remarkable *tour de force* Milton has logically tied these four somewhat antagonistic conceptions into one solid knot; he has done it in six lines, but only because the *Tikunē Zohar* had done it in ten."

1. Pp. 15 ff., above.
2. *Milton, Man and Thinker*, p. 288. See also *Milton and the Zohar, Studies in Philology*, XIX, 136 ff.

His interpretation is as follows: "If we go back to the complete passage in Milton, in its very construction we shall find an exact reproduction of these few lines of the *Zohar*:

Boundless the deep, because I am who fill	When we think that the Holy One . . . is infinite and that he fills every-thing,
Infinitude, nor vacuous the space.	
Though I uncircumscribed myself retire,	it is easily understood that any crea-tion would have been impossible
And put not forth my goodness, which is free	without the *zimzum* ["retraction"] . . . . The Holy One (Blessed be He) has therefore contracted the Holy Light which is his essence;
To act or not. Necessity and Chance Approach not me, and what I will is fate. vii, 168 ff.	not that he diminished himself — God preserve us from such an idea! — being all things, he can neither increase nor decrease.

"In the two texts we find in the same order:

1. *The assertion that God is infinite*, repeated twice — 'I am who fill infinitude' rendering 'the Holy One is infinite,' and 'nor vacuous the space' rendering 'he fills everything';

2. *The idea of 'retraction*,' the English 'retire' rendering *zimzum* ('retrait' in the French of de Pauly), and 'put not forth my goodness' rendering 'contracted the Holy Light,' since 'goodness' and 'Light' are two names of the Shekhina, the essence that plays the principal part in the *Zohar*;

3. *The assertion* that, in spite of this 'retraction,' God remains all powerful, his greatness undiminished.

"It appears, therefore, that the passage from *Paradise Lost* is simply an adaptation of, or properly a sort of free translation from, the passage in the *Tikunē Zohar*. Milton has omitted only the comparison to the cup of water, which was a hindrance to the logical impetuosity of his period." [1]

"This creative liberation can only be accomplished by a 're-traction' of God upon himself: the divinity, as Milton says,

1. *Milton, Man and Thinker*, p. 287.

'retires' its will from certain parts of itself, giving them over, so to speak, to whatever latent impulses remain in them." [1]

Now Saurat's argument rests mainly on his interpretation of the word "retire" as meaning "contract" or "retract." That Milton's "retire" cannot be so interpreted is evident in the light of the Du Bartas passage now to be considered.

We must consider Milton's six lines *in their context.* It is impossible to understand them unless we bear in mind that they are in part a technical answer to a technical question proposed by Adam to Raphael. Adam asks, among other things, the old, old question [2] asked by the commentators on Genesis and others:

> What cause
> *Moved* the Creator, in his holy *rest*
> Through all *eternity, so late* to build
> In Chaos.   vii, 90 ff.

It must be borne in mind also that the question as to the *lateness* of the creation was often accompanied in the Hexaemeral writings by another question — that asked by Du Bartas: "What did God find to do with himself before Creation?" [3] The technical answer given by Du Bartas makes clear these six lines of Milton as the answer to Adam's question. The Du Bartas question and answer are:

> Before all Time, all Matter, Form, and Place,
> God *all in all,* and *all in God it was*:
> *Immutable, immortal, infinite,*
> Incomprehensible, all spirit all *light,*
> All Majestie, all-self-*Omnipotent,*
> *Invisible,* impassive, excellent,
> Pure, wise, just, good, God reign'd alone (*at rest*).
> Thou scoffing atheist, that inquirest what
> The Almighty did before he framed that.   DB, 1 rb

1. *Milton, Man and Thinker,* p. 286.
2. See Robbins, p. 86. He cites Parmenides, Diels, Lucretius, Bruno, Arnold of Chartres, St. Augustine, Milton.
3. Du Bartas, p. 2. As for the frequency of this question among the Hexaemeral writers, see Robbins, pp. 7, 45, 47, 53, 65, 66, 98.

To this question Du Bartas replies that *rest* "before Time was,"
"in eternity," was not idleness but contemplation, and that perhaps God had *meditated* the "idea" of the World, as contrasted
with his active *creating* "in time." The "*in his holy rest,*" as Adam
calls it, was the condition of God, so to speak, naturally. But says
Raphael to Adam, Satan had divested Heaven of one third of its
beings. Nature abhors a vacuum. God, to replace these fallen
angels, *is moved* to create other beings, and a habitation for them
out of chaos. Raphael is explaining how God exercised this active
creative process as in contrast to his accustomed principle of being, — *at rest.* God, however, exercises his creative faculties as to
only a limited portion of chaos in order to make the world. As to
the other portion of chaos, upon that he *does not* "put forth his
goodness." "Put forth his goodness" is synonymous in the commentators with *create.*[1] As to these other parts of chaos, he "retires" — not in the sense of contracts, but in the sense of remaining in his state "*at rest.*" The creative process among the Hexaemeral writers is clearly an *expanding* not a *contracting* process.[2] It
is an encroachment on chaos, not a retiring from it.

The last lines of the six,

> *Necessity* and *Chance*
> Approach not me.

are not to be interpreted as by Saurat. "Chance" is dismissed by
Du Bartas in the second line of his great work as not being the
"cause" Adam inquires about:[3] "World not eternall, nor by
Chance compos'd." That there was no "necessity" for God's
creating the world is another Hexaemeral commonplace.[4] He does
not need to create since he is already perfect.

1. Robbins, pp. 45, 47, 53, 65, 74, 87.
2. Robbins, pp. 4, 5 note, 39, 52, 66, 74, 83.
3. See also for "chance" as not one of the causes of creation, Robbins, pp. 24, 47.
4. See Robbins, p. 87.

The six lines, then, reduced to prose would comprise the follow-ing statement of God the Father (contemplative) to God the Son (active): "Go forth and create the world out of a portion of chaos. Put an outer shell around it to protect it against the inroads of this chaos. So bound the World. Chaos itself is boundless because I am infinite, am everywhere extending to all points of it and fill it. Think not that the uncreated part of chaos is a vacuum. I fill it, 'uncircumscribed.' I am everywhere, although I do not everywhere exercise the active principle of being on all chaos, not putting forth my goodness as to all chaos, but, as to the greater part of chaos, *remaining*, as I have been from all eternity, *at rest*, 'retired.'"

Elsewhere in discussing Milton's conception of God, Saurat says,[1] "To Milton God is infinite, unknowable, unmanifested. This is the 'en-Sof,' the Endless of the Zohar." And again[2] he quotes in this connection:

> Thee, Father first they sung, *Omnipotent,*
> *Immutable, Immortal, Infinite,*
> Eternal King; . . .
> *Fountain of light*, thyself *invisible.*   *P.L.*, iii, 372 ff.

But Du Bartas is beforehand here, one entire line passing from him to Milton:[3]

> Before all Time, all Matter, Form, and Place,
> God *all in all*, and *all in God it was*:
> *Immutable, immortal, infinite,*
> Incomprehensible, all spirit all *light,*
> *All Majestie*, all-self-*Omnipotent,*
> *Invisible.*   DB, 1 rb

Saurat calls attention[4] to

> Because I am who fill
> Infinitude.   *P.L.*, vii, 168

---

1. *Milton and the Zohar, Studies in Philology*, XIX, 143.
2. *Milton, Man and Thinker*, p. 122.
3. Noted by Candy, *Notes and Queries*, CLVIII (1930), 93 ff.
4. *Milton, Man and Thinker*, p. 115.

as evidence of Milton's Pantheism. The lines above quoted from Du Bartas say this clearly: "not as *all filling*" says Du Bartas elsewhere of the angels; "God alone is so." [1] Du Bartas, moreover, repeats this idea frequently.[2] As evidence that Milton conceived that God actually created the world immediately, but interpreted the creation as extending through six days because human beings cannot comprehend the idea of an immediate creation, Saurat quotes: [3]

> Immediate are the acts of God . . .
> . . . but to human ears
> . . . .
> So told as earthly notion can receive.   *P.L.*, vii, 176 ff.

If Saurat considers this an evidence of Milton's lack of orthodoxy, then Du Bartas and many another before him were unorthodox also: Du Bartas says: "His Word and Deed in an instant wrought." [4] Du Bartas says elsewhere that the world was *not* created "all at once." An analysis of the Fall of Man reveals that it consists largely of the triumph of the passions over Reason, says Saurat.[5] The entire system of the Fall and its results elaborately worked out by Du Bartas will be given in Chapter IV in order to show that Milton follows closely the scheme of Du Bartas. Attention may here be called, however, to what Du Bartas says in connection with the creation of Adam:

> Also thou plantedst *th' Intellectuall Pow'r*
> In th' highest stage of all this stately Bowr,
> That thence it might (as from a Cittadell)
> Command the members that too-oft *rebell*

---

1. Du Bartas, 154 lc.
2. Du Bartas, 11 lc, 140 rb.
3. *Milton, Man and Thinker*, p. 115.
4. Du Bartas, 53 l. For Medieval and early references to this idea, see p. 19, note 5, above.
5. *Milton, Man and Thinker*, pp. 150 ff.

> *Against* his *Rule*: and that our *Reason*, there
> Keeping continuall Garrison (as 't were)
> Might Avarice, Envie, and Pride subdue,
> Lust, Gluttony, Wrath, Sloath, and all their Crew
> Of factious Commons, that *still strive to gaine*
> *The* golden *Scepter from their Soverain.*   DB, 53 rc

And he follows this in *The Furies* [1] with

> And now (alas!) through our fond Parents Fall
> They [the animals] of our slaves are grown our tyrants all.
>   DB, 97 lc

and proceeds to the "passions":

> But, lo! *foure Captains* far more fierce and eager,
> That on all sides the Spirit it selfe beleaguer,
> Whose Constancy they shake, and soon by treason
> *Draw the blinde Judgement from the rule of Reason:*
> *Opinions* issue; which (though selfe unseen)
> Make through the Body their fell motions seen.   DB, 100 rc

Then follows the ascendency of the passions over man after Reason is dethroned — Sorrow, "excessive Joy," Feare, Desire, and others.

Saurat calls attention to Milton's words as to marriage legitimizing the desires:

> Our maker bids increase, who bids abstain,
> But our destroyer, foe to God and man.   *P.L.*, iv, 748, 749

Du Bartas follows his hymn in praise of marriage (which somewhat resembles Milton's after the creation of Adam and Eve) by saying that "increase" is

> Rather *commanded* then allowed.   DB, 155 lc

Eve's inferiority to Adam is stressed by Saurat.[2] Her inferiority is definitely emphasized in Du Bartas. His language as to why the Serpent showed wisdom in approaching Eve is even more emphatic than Milton's:

1. Du Bartas, 97 lc and 98 lc.
2. *Milton, Man and Thinker*, pp. 160, 161 ff.

> Namely, poor Woman, wavering, weak, unwise,
> Light, credulous news-lover, giv'n to lies.   DB, 91 rb

Saurat mentions the conception in the *Zohar*, as in Milton, "that there is in the Fall much that is good." [1] Du Bartas is very close to Milton here, arriving at the conclusion, as Milton does, as a result of the discussion of free will: [2]

> Making thee blessed more since thine offence
> Than in thy primer happy innocence.

NICOLSON

In a series of three articles [3] Miss Marjorie H. Nicolson relates Milton to the intellectual currents of his day. Perhaps no other modern scholar has succeeded in interpreting Milton's God with more vital significance. "This idea of the rational relation between the faculties in the human and the divine nature is fundamental to Milton's defense of God in *Paradise Lost*. Take it away, allow the Will of God the supremacy, and the argument becomes meaningless." [4] This statement renders philosophically attractive what to the critics has hitherto been the most deadly, wooden part of the great epic. In this and in many other regards Milton scholarship is under obligation to Miss Nicolson. All of her articles must be read, however, against a background of Du Bartas. All studies of Cabbalistic doctrines as related to Milton must reckon with Du Bartas who was, as he himself says, "by Tradition Cabalistik taught." [5]

1. *Studies in Philology*, XIX, 149; many of the scholars now interested in the sources of Milton's thought find this idea elsewhere than in Milton. See p. 22, note 10, above.

2. Du Bartas, 93 rc.

3. *The Spirit World of Milton and More, Studies in Philology*, XXII (1925), 433 ff.; *Milton and Hobbes, Studies in Philology*, XXIII (1926), 405 ff.; *Milton and the Conjectura Cabbalistica, Philological Quarterly*, VI (1927), 1 ff.

4. *Studies in Philology*, XXIII, 431.

5. Du Bartas, 136 lc.

A rapid survey of some of the matters treated in these three articles will make this very clear. Miss Nicolson, discussing the Nature of Angels, says, "They can and do change their shape by the imperium of the will." "When they are bound on messages from God, for instance, they appear now one way, now another. Moreover, the baser spirits frequently descend to animal shapes in order to carry our their purposes." [1] "Intelligential substances require food"; [2] "they have moral choice"; [3] "Milton's heaven resounds to the music of the heavenly host"; [4] "both of them [Milton and More] hold that the spirits are the messengers of God." [5] As to these matters notice the following passages from Du Bartas:

> For Angels being mere Intelligences
>
> .   .   .   .   .   .
>
> To treat with us they put our Nature-on;
> And take a body fit to exercise
> The charge they have, which runnes, *and feeds* and flies;
> Dures during their Commission.
>
> But always in some place are Angels.
>
> So, visibly those bodies move, and oft
> By word of Mouth bring *arrands* from aloft,
> And *eat* with us.   DB, 154 lc
>
> Whether, This-Day, God made you, Angels,
>
> .   .   .   .
>
> I am resolv'd that once th' Omnipotent
> Created you immortall, innocent,
> Good, faire, and *free*; in briefe, of Essence, such
> As from his own differ'd not very much.   DB, 6 lc
>
> With willing speed they every moment go
> Whither the breath of divine grace doth blow.   DB, 7 lc

---

1. *Studies in Philology*, xxii, 438.
2. The same, xxii, 440.
3. The same, xxii, 447.
4. The same, xxii, 448.
5. The same, xxii, 449.

Du Bartas follows this last passage with a long list of the divine commissions which specific angels are sent upon.

> So, these Seducers can grow great or small,
> Or round, or square, or straight, or short, or tall
> As fits the passions they are moved by.   DB, 90 rb

Then follows a long disquisition as to the various shapes assumed by Satan, similar in a multitude of particulars to the same identical matters in Milton.[1]

In her second study [2] Miss Nicolson says:

"With the English Platonists, Milton shares the Stoic exaltation of Reason, in which he finds the chief gift of God to man; originally possessed by all men equally, the light of Reason becomes dim only when man allows his passions to usurp the authority of Reason. . . . *Sin* to Milton consists in a reversal on the part of man of the natural faculties; appetite triumphs over will, will over Reason, and man, the image of God, becomes no more than a beast." [3] As to all this, compare Du Bartas when he describes the creation of Adam:

> Also thou plantedst th' Intellectuall Pow'r
> In th' highest stage of all this stately Bowr,
> That thence it might (as from a Cittadell)
> Command the members that too-oft rebell
> *Against his Rule*: and that our *Reason*, there
> Keeping continuall Garrison . . .
> Might Avarice, Envie, and Pride subdue,
> . . . and all their Crew
> Of factious Commons that still *strive to gaine*
> *The* golden *Scepter* from their Soverain.   DB, 53 rc

> For, God had not depriv'd that primer season
> The sacred lamp and light of learned Reason:
> Mankinde was then a thousand fold more wise
> Than now: blinde Errour had not bleard his eyes.   DB, 83 rc

---

1. See for details p. 72, below.
2. *Studies in Philology*, XXIII, (1926), 405 ff.
3. The same, XXIII, 418.

In *The Furies* (the Third Part of the First Day of the Second Week), not only all the *passions* but all the other forces inimical to man are let loose upon the human race as the result of the Fall and the consequent dethronement of Reason. The details are followed in many cases with obvious interest by Milton throughout Book ix of *Paradise Lost*.[1]

In her study of Milton and Hobbes Miss Nicolson discusses the doctrine of free will in Milton and Hobbes. Du Bartas enters into a long discussion of free will in his justification of the ways of God to Man, and his language is strangely similar to Milton's.[2] However, the discussion of free will is too much of a commonplace to justify any inference as to relationship.[3] Still it is worth noting that Du Bartas, like Milton, urges as the final argument that, but for man's fall through free will, he would not have arrived at a state superior to his original state of innocence in Paradise:

> But that thou didst erre,
> Christ had not come.
>
> .   .   .   .
>
> Making thee blessed more since thine offence
> Than in thy primer happy innocence.   DB, 93 rc

Miss Nicolson argues that *Paradise Lost* was a reply to atheism. Du Bartas has a splendid arch atheist in his work in the person of Cham. In his defiance of God Cham is not, of course, Milton's Satan, but he suggests Satan's dynamic strength. And his bold attack on God is followed (which is much more to our purpose) by an elaborate statement, running through hundreds of lines,[4] of what Du Bartas calls the thirteen answers to atheism. It is particularly interesting to compare Miss Nicolson's statement of the unjust God with Cham's:

1. See ll. 1123 ff. See below, pp. 104 ff.
2. Du Bartas, 93.
3. See p. 15, note 1; p. 17, note 7; pp. 69 ff.
4. Du Bartas, pp. 114, 115, 116.

If God could have made the nature of man other than it is, and did consciously, with his foreknowledge, make him to fall, then he is not God but devil or the bored deity of Bertrand Russell's Free Man's Worship.[1]

Cham's words of scorn about God are strong enough even for the temper of those moderns who are continually insisting that we have not been treated fairly in the biological scheme of things:

> Will you always forge yourselfe a Censor?
>
> . . . .
>
> A barbarous Butcher, that with bloody knife
> Threats day and night your grievous-guilty life?
>
> . . . .
>
> Faining a God . . .
> Fainter than Women, fiercer than a Beast.
> Who, tender-hearted, weeps at others weeping,
> Wails others woes. . . .
>
> . . . .
>
> In manly breast a woman's heart possesses:
> And who (remorse-less) lets at any season
> The stormy tide of rage transport his reason.
>
> . . . .
>
> Hide's a Bear heart under a humane shape.
>
> . . . .
>
> O goodly Justice! one or two of us
> Have sinn'd perhaps, and mov'd his anger thus;
> All bear the pain, yea even the Innocent.   DB, 114 rc

To this matter of atheism Du Bartas returns again and again. Indeed, one of his main reasons for writing is to confute atheists. In thousands of lines he proves what Bacon suggests in a sentence: God's "ordinary works refute it." [2]

In Miss Nicolson's third study, *Milton and The Conjectura Cabbalistica*,[3] Milton's relations to Cabbalistic doctrines is investigated further. It may be interesting to note how important it is to have Du Bartas in mind in connection with certain parts of her discussion.

---

1. *Studies in Philology*, XXIII, 431.   2. *Of Atheism*.
3. *Philological Quarterly*, VI, 1 ff.

guage warranting the conclusion that Milton had read and remembered Du Bartas in these connections. Larson calls attention
to the treatment of the creation of the world in Servetus and
Milton. By this time it will have become apparent that this
matter of the creation is so frequently to be found in writings of
both the Renaissance and the Middle Ages, in such diverse types of
literature,[1] that it is hazardous to conclude that any of these treatments had a direct influence upon Milton unless its wording is
very similar to his.

Larson quotes [2] Milton's Platonism —

> How good, how fair
> Answering his great idea —

as showing similarity between the Platonism of Servetus and of
Milton. But Du Bartas is clearly in point here:

> It may be also, that he meditated
> The World's Idea, ere it was created.   DB, 2 lc

In this passage it must be noted also that it is the "Word" in Du
Bartas as in Servetus which does, or who does, the creating.[3]
Larson frequently calls attention to the conception of the "Word"
and its functions — "how it reduces a portion of God's material
aspect to form and order"; "how it may be interpreted"; "the
sound of his voice," how it is the "visible," instrumental side of
God to man; — and to other qualities of the Word as reflected
in Milton and Servetus, as for example the distinction between
the Word as Son of God and the Christ manifestation of it.[4] Du
Bartas's work contains numerous references to the fact that it is
the "word" which has the creative function:

1. See above, pp. 16 ff.
2. *P.M.L.A.*, xli, 904.
3. Du Bartas, p. 140 rb.
4. *P.M.L.A.*, xli, 903 ff.; for the prevalence of these conceptions see above, p. 17,
notes 1 and 2.

God *reign'd alone* (at rest)
Himselfe alone.

Alone he liv'd not; for his Son and Spirit
Were with him aye, equal in Might and Merit.
For sans Beginning, Seed and Mother tender,
This great World's Father [the Word]
    he did first ingender.

But, adds Du Bartas, realizing the mystical nature of his subject,

Soft, soft, my Muse, launch not into the Deep,
Sound not this Sea.   DB, 2 lb

Perhaps he is distinguishing between God without the Word before
"time" and the Word first of created things "in Time." Larson
very pertinently calls attention to a possible confusion in *Paradise
Lost* of God the Father and God the Word in the words of the
Creator to Adam:[1]

What think'st thou then of me and this my state?

.   .   .   .

    who am alone
From all eternity; for none I know
Second to me or like, *equal much less.*
How have I then with whom to hold converse,
Save with the creatures which I made, and those
To me inferior, infinite descents
Beneath what other creatures are to thee?   vIII, 403 ff.

These words seem reminiscent of the lines just quoted from Du
Bartas.[2] It is peculiarly important to notice Larson's observation
that the creative side of God is called by Milton the oracle, the
voice, the word, the speech, of God,[3] because they are among the
most striking of those wonderful synonyms in *Paradise Lost* by
means of which Milton secures infinite variety in his numerous

1. *P.M.L.A.*, xLI, 927, 928.
2. That Milton and Du Bartas are at one as to the Word, its powers, the time of creation, and various other matters connected with it, this study makes no claim.
3. *P.M.L.A.*, xLI, p. 920.

references to the Son of God. Notice the same terms in Du Bartas, whose synonyms for God the Father, God the Son, and God the Holy Ghost, if one cares to list them and compare them with Milton's, will show a most remarkable correspondence:

> I wote not what great *Word he uttered*
> From his sacred *mouth*; which summon'd in a Masse
> Whats' ever now the Heav'n's wide arms embrace.   DB, 3 lb

> How, when the *Mouth Divine*
> Op'ned, (to each his proper place t' assigne),
> Fire flew to Fire, Water to Water slid.   DB, 11 rb

Finally Larson calls attention [1] to the fact that "the Father always remains inscrutable and unknowable" and quotes the passage from Milton iii, 373 ff. beginning, "Immutable, Immortal, Infinite." But in this case, as I have already shown,[2] Milton has actually borrowed an entire line from Du Bartas.[3] Throughout Larson's study one must keep Du Bartas always in mind as the possible intermediary between Servetus and Milton in many cases and the certain source of Milton in others.

E. N. S. Thompson

Mr. E. N. S. Thompson's study of *Milton's Knowledge of Geography* [4] makes no mention of Du Bartas. Doubtless the conclusions of that article would not be materially different had Du Bartas been considered. Still, if one went no further than *The Colonies*,[5] one would find that the descendants of Sem, Cham, Japeth are followed by Du Bartas through two hundred geographical localities. Here, within five folio pages, time and space are ransacked for geographical details. Is it conceivable that

1. P.M.L.A., xli, p. 926.
2. P. 42, above. Noted also by Candy. See above, p. 16, note 1.
3. L. 45 of Sylvester's Du Bartas.
4. *Studies in Philology*, xvi, 148 ff.
5. The Third Part of the Second Day of the Second Week of Sylvester, pp. 127 ff.

Milton, interested in geography as he was, should not have been
attracted by these pages? Column follows column resounding
with proper names rich in story and poetical allusion. Here one
finds, for example:

> Where stately Ob, the King of Rivers, roars,
> In Scythian seas voyding his violent load,
>   . . . sayling broad
> To Malaco; Moluques Isles, that bear
> Cloves and canele; well tempered Sumater
>   . . . and the golden streams
> Of Bisnagar and Zeilan bearing gemms: DB, 128 lt

Here are

> *Odours from Arabia come:*
> From India, drugs, rich Gemms and Ivorie:
> From Syria, Mummy: black-red Ebony
> From burning Chus: from Peru, Pearl and Gold.   DB, 133 lt

This, with Du Bartas's "*Saban odours*," [1] is certainly worth noting
in connection with the passage quoted by Thompson [2] from
Paradise Lost,

> *Sabæan odours* from the spicy shore
> Of Araby the Blest.   iv, 162–163

Du Bartas refers to many of the countries, mountains and rivers
mentioned by Milton. And with Milton's epic devices for shorten-
ing long lists, — such as "The rest were long to tell," [3] or "I might
relate of thousands and their names eternize here on earth," [4] —
one may compare the lines of Du Bartas:

> I could derive the lineall Descents
> Of all our Sires: and name you every Prince
> Of every Province . . .
>
> .   .   .   .
>
> Yea, sing the World's so divers populations.   DB, 128 rt

---

1. Du Bartas, 208 lt.
2. *Studies in Philology*, XVI, 162.
3. *P.L.*, i, 507.
4. The same, vi, 373–374.

In spite of this declaration of restraint upon his encyclopædic knowledge, Du Bartas proceeds exhaustively to enumerate many of the tribes of mankind and their places of abode. Occasionally in doing this he resembles Milton. For example:

> the Goth, who whilom issuing forth
> From the cold *frozen* Ilands of the *North*
> (follows a description of his wanderings through various lands)

> Then comes to Gaul: thence repulst, his Legions
> Rest ever since upon the Spanish Regions.   DB, 129 lc

One hundred and fifty lines later he says of the sons of Sem,

> The sons of these, '*like flowing waters,*' *spred*
> O'r all the Country.   DB, 130 lc

All of which may have resulted in Milton's extraordinary account of the migration of a great nation:

> A multitude, like which the populous *North*
> Poured never from her *frozen* loins, to pass
> Rhene or the Danaw, when her barbarous sons
> Came *like* a *deluge* on the South, and *spread*
> Beneath Gibraltar to the Libyan sands.   *P.L.*, i, 351 ff.

Here also Milton's "Delos floating once" (x, 296) occurs in the form

> Delos floating on the Seas.   DB, 130 rc

It is particularly important to bear Du Bartas in mind in connection with an idea which Thompson traces to Aristotle, since Du Bartas declares that he is "treading the way that Aristotle went" [1] in another connection. "Closely connected with Milton's general interest in geography was his belief in the influence of climate on human character. The idea was by no means his own. In his *Politics* Aristotle had taught that 'those who live in cold climate . . . are full of spirit but wanting in intelligence . . .

---

1. Du Bartas, 17 lb.

whereas the natives of Asia are intelligent.'" [1] In his great geographical passage [2] Du Bartas stops for a long and clear disquisition on this identical theme, saying among other things in his list of distinctions:

> The Southern-man, who, quick and curious witty,
>
> . . . can hardly be surprised
>
> With Vulgar Knowledge.
>
> The Northern-man whose wit in's Fingers settles.   DB, 132 lb

And the lines quoted by Thompson in connection with Milton's impression of the effect which climate has upon his own muse in his Urania motif at the beginning of Book ix of *Paradise Lost* —

> Unless an age too late, or cold
> Climate, or years, damp my intended wing
> Depressed —

are, strangely enough, apparently influenced by lines from Du Bartas in similar vein, without reference to climate:

> Mine humbled Muse flag in a lowly flight;
> Blame these sad Times ingratefull cruelty,
> My household cares, my health's infirmity,
> My drooping sorrows . . .
> My bitter suits, and other bitter crosses.   DB, 113 lb

FLETCHER

Harris Francis Fletcher's studies in *Milton's Rabbinical Readings* [3] sheds light on many of the points investigated by the recent movement in Milton scholarship and upon many important points not investigated by other scholars. Nevertheless, even this work, a contribution of outstanding value, must be examined with Du

---

1. *Studies in Philology*, XVI, 170.
2. Du Bartas, 132.
3. University of Illinois Press, Urbana, 1930.

Bartas in mind before one accepts Fletcher's conclusions. If the reader will glance back at Chapter II, he will notice how necessary it is to consider other sources than those investigated by Fletcher in regard to such matters particularly as the creation *ex nihilo*,[1] the nature of Chaos,[2] the Holy Spirit, as "the impregnating" force in creation,[3] the *immediate* nature of creation,[4] the stages of creation represented by six days,[5] *matter and form*,[6] the "abyss," [7] *matter comes from God and is good*,[8] *no space no time before creation*,[9] *Adam made outside Eden and then placed there*,[10] Light created before the Sun and afterwards the greater part of it condensed into Sun,[11] Adam's high degree of intelligence before the Fall,[12] his naming of animals without education,[13] *the relation of Adam's intelligence to the Fall*,[14] man's state after the Fall *superior to his state of innocence in some regards*.[15]

Though many of the ideas and approaches to the ideas in *Paradise Lost* considered by Fletcher as perhaps determined by Milton's rabbinical readings are not to be found in Du Bartas, a great number of them are to be found there, and sometimes in such form as to make it next to impossible to deny that they were definitely affected by Du Bartas.

One of the most important of these concerns the nature of Chaos. How Du Bartas influenced Milton's treatment of Chaos has already been made clear in opposition to Greenlaw's claims for Spenser.[16] Fletcher's study of the "impregnating" nature of the

1. *Milton's Rabbinical Readings*, pp. 82, 83, 86.
2. Pp. 84, 85.
3. Pp. 90, 91, 118, 124, 126, 127, 130, 143.
4. Pp. 122, 124, 125, 127, 143, 148, 149, 183.
5. Pp. 124, 125, 127, 128, 147, 149, 153.
6. Pp. 130, 144, 145.   7. Pp. 130, 135.   8. P. 144.
9. Pp. 148, 155.   10. Pp. 168, 169.   11. P. 149.
12. Pp. 187, 188, 189, 190, 191.
13. Pp. 187, 188, 189.   14. P. 191.   15. P. 204.
16. See above, pp. 30, 31, and p. 18, notes 6, 7, 8, 9.

Holy Spirit in the process of creation must be read in connection both with the other treatments of this subject [1] and particularly with that passage in Du Bartas best known to Milton-Du Bartas controversy:

> Or, as a Hen . . . would hatch a *Brood*
>
> .   .   .   .
>
> . . . and with her *lively heat*,
> . . . doth live birds beget:
> . . . seemed the *Spirit* Eternall
> To *brood* upon this Gulf . . .
> *Quickning the parts*.   DB, 4 lc

Surely this is close enough to Milton's

> On the watery calm
> His *brooding* wings *the Spirit of God* outspread,
> And vital virtue *infused*, and *vital warmth*,
> *Throughout the fluid mass*.   *P.L.*, vii, 234 ff.

and

> Dove-like sat'st *brooding* on the vast *Abyss*
> And *mad'st it pregnant*.   *P.L.*, i, 21–22

The conception is so ancient [2] that, unless supported by extraordinary verbal similarities, it weighs little in determining relations.

Fletcher [3] notes that "time" came with the circling of the planets and quotes:

> Let them [the lights] be for signs,
> For seasons and for days
>   and circling years   *P.L.*, vii, 341–342
>
> They, [the stars] as they move
> Their *Starry dance* in numbers that *compute*
> *Days*, *months*, and *years*,   *P.L.*, iii, 579 ff.

Is it possible to doubt that Milton had Du Bartas in mind here?

1. See above, p. 17, note 5.
2. Philo Judaeus (A.D. *ca.* 40). See above, p. 17, note 5.
3. *Milton's Rabbinical Readings*, p. 155.

> New Heav'ns, new Stars, whose whirling courses
> With constant windings, tho contrary ways should,
> *Mark the true mounds of Years* and *Months* and *Daies*?
>
> DB, 56 rb

> But in the instant when Time first became.
>   . . . for the course
>
>   .   .   .   .
>
> Of Ages, Times, and Seasons is confin'd
> By th' ordred *Dance* unto the *Stars*.
>
> DB, 1 rb

Fletcher cites [1] Rashi's commentary as to Milton's

>   over all the face of Earth
> Main Ocean flowed.   *P.L.*, vii, 278–279

Du Bartas has

> And all the Earth . . . a dull Pond abid.   DB, 21 rt

and he proceeds to describe the assembling of the waters in a style which, as I shall later show, influenced Milton very definitely.[2] Rashi's commentary is cited [3] also in connection with the idea that Adam was created outside of the Garden of Eden and afterwards placed in it. Fletcher suggests that the "chief basis for this was doubtless Biblical," but that the idea of the "persuasion" of Adam to enter was supplied by Rashi. Now Du Bartas has Adam created outside and afterwards placed inside Eden, but he assigns a very definite reason for this change:

> Now Heav'ns eternall all-fore-seeing King,
>
>   .   .   .   .
>
> Thought good, *that man* (having yet spirit sound-stated)
> Should *dwel elsewhere*, than where he was created;
> *That he might know, he did not hold this place*
> *By Naturees right*, but by meer gift and grace.
>
> DB, 83 and 84 lt

A portion of this thought Milton transmutes into wonderful poetry when Raphael tells Adam that God created a wide Universe:

1. *Milton's Rabbinical Readings*, p. 168.   2. See below, pp. 86 ff.
3. *Milton's Rabbinical Readings*, p. 169.

That Man may know he dwells not in his own.   *P.L.*, viii, 103

Rashi is, as Fletcher maintains, in point in connection with Milton's emphasizing the inferiority of Eve to Adam,[1] but Du Bartas must certainly be considered also. He remarks that Satan chose Eve rather than Adam as the subject of his temptation:

> Namely, poor Woman, wavering, weak, unwise,
> Light, credulous news-lover, giv'n to lies.   DB, 91 rb

Fletcher [2] cites Rashi as an aid to the interpreting of Milton's Sun which

> *in a cloudy tabernacle*
> Sojourned the while.   *P.L.*, vii, 248–249

But Du Bartas is of immense importance here as the medium through which a point known to commentaries on Genesis [3] got into Milton's discussion of the original creation of light before it gathered in the sun:

> Whether about the vast confused Crowd,
> For twice six-hours he spread a *shining Cloud*,   DB, 5 rt

especially when one remembers that the words of Milton immediately preceding Fletcher's quotation are

> *Sphered* in a *radiant cloud*, for yet the sun
> Was not.   *P.L.*, vii, 247–248

Fletcher devotes several pages to the discussion of the fact that in both Rashi and Milton "Adam was immediately possessed of a perfect knowledge of nature." [4] The results are illuminating, but one should bear in mind how common the conception is in the literature of the Middle Ages and the Renaissance.[5] The idea of Adam's intelligence, especially in relation to his ability to name the

---

1. The same, pp. 178 ff.   2. The same, p. 149.
3. See Robbins, p. 80.   4. *Milton's Rabbinical Readings*, pp. 189 ff.
5. See above, p. 21, note 6.

animals, as discussed by Fletcher in connection with Rashi, began certainly as early as Philo Judaeus [1] and occurs in Du Bartas. Adam's "sudden apprehension," cited by Fletcher,[2] was well known by the thirteenth century. It appears elaborately worked out, in Adam's relation to the Fall, in that compendium of general knowledge, *L'Image du Monde*,[3] translated by Caxton 1497, in order to educate Englishmen, as *The Mirrour of the World*.[4] Even Grafton's *Chronicle at Large* (1569) begins with the statement that Adam was "learned and seen in all the liberall Arts and Sciences. He was also endowed with the knowledge of all Herbs, Trees, Metalls, Stones, Birds, Beast, Fowles, Fishes, Worms, and of all other creatures." But it is highly significant that Milton certainly ran across the following passage in Du Bartas:

> For, God had not depriv'd that primer season
> The sacred lamp and light of learned Reason:
> Mankinde was then a thousand fold more wise
> Then now.   DB, 83 rc

As already noted,[5] Du Bartas has described how God in creating Adam made Reason predominant over all the faculties. The dethronement of Reason, the rise of other faculties in the Soul, the effects of Adam's sin even on the Cosmos and on earth, as elaborately worked out by Du Bartas in the *Imposture* and *The Furies*, will be considered in Chapter IV,[6] where Books ix, x, and xi of *Paradise Lost* are treated in detail. Finally, the entire matter of the Plan of Creation in Milton and Ben Gerson [7] has to be studied in connection with the contributions to Milton by Du Bartas as

1. *De Opificio Mundi*, 49, 7; 52; 8 ff. (Opera ed. Cohn and Wendland, 1, 52). See Robbins, pp. 33 ff.
2. P. 188.
3. Ed. by O. H. Prior, Lausanne, 1913, p. 180.
4. Ed. by O. H. Prior, E.E.T.S., 1913.
5. P. 21, above; see also pp. 28 ff.
6. Pp. 104 ff.
7. Pp. 91 ff.

explained and developed in Chapter IV,[1] where the extraordinary similarity of Book vii and Du Bartas are treated. These are only a few of the matters discussed by Fletcher which must be studied in Du Bartas before one can come to any definite conclusion as to which had the more direct influence upon Milton, his rabbinical readings or Du Bartas.

1. The same.

Chapter IV

DU BARTAS AND THE TWELVE BOOKS OF
PARADISE LOST

THE preceding chapters have attempted to clear the ground for the presentation of the Du Bartas material as it bears upon *Paradise Lost* book by book. In many instances where material is presented from Du Bartas, as Chapter II makes clear, no definite claim is made as to Milton's direct indebtedness. These doubtful passages are to be considered merely for what they are worth along with the other treatments of these themes investigated by modern Milton scholarship in various sources and analogues. In many instances, however, the treatment by Du Bartas of material treated also by Milton is similar in multiplicity of detail and in exact correspondence of expression. When the evidence is finally all in, the matter is still left in the form of a question for the reader to answer for himself: Is there any other epic material in the Renaissance so important as that of Du Bartas in determining the substance and the form of *Paradise Lost*?

Book I

Books i and ii of *Paradise Lost* are generally regarded as the finest part of the poem. Although this is of course largely a matter of taste, the study of *Paradise Lost* in its relation to *The Divine Weekes and Workes* may prove of interest in this regard. These two books and Book vi show less substantial use of Du Bartas than the other books. Yet even in Books i and ii the influence of Du Bartas is obvious. It consists mostly in unquestionable verbal reminiscences.

After the first thirty-five lines the elements in this first book for which Milton is celebrated as a poet are not found in Du Bartas. His Satan of Book i is not the Satan of Du Bartas's *Imposture*, however much the Satan conception in some of the later books may be traced to Du Bartas. But the following lines from the invocation have influenced *Paradise Lost* too plainly in the opening of his epic to be omitted here.

Milton		Du Bartas	
Sing, Heavenly Muse, that on the secret top		O sacred Muse! that on the *double Mount*	
Of Oreb, or of Sinai. . . .	i, 6–7	. . . bindest not thy singers, But, on Mount Sion	
		. . . . . .	
Instruct me, *for thou know'st*;	i, 19	*Tell (for, thou know'st)* what *sacred mystery*	
		Under this shadow doth in secret lie?	
		. . . . . .	
till one greater Man [Christ]		. . . *that Prince* [Christ] . . . ordain'd to dye, Upon Mount Sion:	
		. . . . . .	
Restore us, and regain the blissful seat [*Eden*].	i, 4–5	*Restores us Eden's key.*	DB 163 rc
Instruct me, for thou know'st.	i, 19	*Instruct my spirit*, and give my tongue smooth scope.	DB 89 rb
What in *me* is *dark Illumine* i, 22, 23 Invoke thy aid to my *adventurous song.*	i, 13	Drive the *darknesse forth* Which blindeth *me:* that my *adventrous Rime* . . .	DB, 127 rc
. . . *O Spirit* . . .			
. . . thou from the first Wast present, and, with mighty wings outspread		So did God's *Spirit* delight . . . To move itselfe upon the floting Masse.	DB, 4 lt

Dove-like sat'st *brooding* on *the vast*
   Abyss

And mad'st it pregnant.   i, 17 ff.   . . . that fain would hatch a Brood
                      Sits close thereon, and with her lively
                        heat,
                      . . . doth live birds beget
                      . . . seemed the *Spirit Eternall*
                      To *brood* upon this Gulf. . . . DB, 4 lt

   the vast Abyss   i, 21   . . . *the vaste abyss.*   DB, 161 lc

There are, in addition, a few touches in Book i which should be noted in connection with Du Bartas. For example:

        A hill   So shall you see a Cloud-crown'd
Torn from Pelorus, or the shattered   *Hill* . . .
   side   *Torn from a greater.*   DB, 181 lb
Of thundering *Ætna.*   i, 231 ff.

Or seventy-eight lines later:

The sojourners of Goshen, who beheld   . . . *Jacob's heirs thus rescu'd from*
                                annoy;
From the safe shore their floating car-   *Seeing the Sea to take their cause in*
   cases   *hand,*
And broken chariot-wheels; so thick   *And their dead Foes shuffled upon the*
   bestrown.   i, 309 ff.   *sand;*
                                  Their shields, and staves, and chariots
                                    (all to-tore)
                                  Floating about, and flung upon the
                                  shore;   DB, 171 rc

Strangely enough the description of Tubal Cain, with the account of his discovery of iron in the earth and his fashioning it to the invention of the mechanic arts, which is to be used in the same connection in Book xi (where Milton's "a sweaty reaper," whom we now know from Du Bartas to be Tubal Cain, is actually described among the visions of Adam in his trance), is used in Book i in recounting the discovery by the devils of metal in the bowels of Hell. The discovery of iron is as follows in Du Bartas:

A second multitude
With wondrous art founded the massy
   ore,
Severing each kind, and *scummed the*
   bullion-dross.
A third as soon had formed within the
   ground
A various mould, and from the boiling
   cells
By strange conveyance filled each hollow
   nook:
As in an *organ,* from one blast of wind,
To many *a row of pipes the sound-*
   board breathes.   i, 702 ff.

An iron River rowls along the Plain:
              DB, 107 rt

In two square creases of unequall sizes
To turn to Iron streamlings he devises;
Cold, takes them thence; then *off the*
   dross he rakes,   DB, 107 rc

And grown more cunning,
   hollow things he formeth.
No time lost Jubal: th' un-full *Harmony*
Of uneven Hammers, beating diversly,
Wakens the tunes that his sweet num-
   bery soule
The birth (some think) learn'd of the
   warbling Pole.   DB, 107 rb

We note that music and the mechanic arts are blended in both Du Bartas and Milton.

Book II

Upon *Paradise Lost* ii, even less of the influence of Du Bartas is to be detected than upon the first book. Of the grand imaginative conceptions of Satan and his peers, of Sin and Death, and of the magnificently sombre background of Hell against which they are cast, there is scarcely a trace. Grotius or Vondel is far more in point here than Du Bartas. But even upon these, Milton's, most supremely successful efforts in poetry, one must concede, after careful examination, impressions from Du Bartas. It is here that one runs across Milton's first detailed description of the qualities of Chaos. And inasmuch as here, as in the other passages in other books, Milton is so plainly affected by Du Bartas's handling of this theme, it seems advisable to consider them all together at this point.[1] It is deeply interesting to observe how the crude and

---

1. After this book was completed there appeared in *Studies in Philology* (vol. xxx, pp. 133 ff.) *A Medieval Commonplace in Spenser's Cosmology* by Raymond Tuve. The Spenserian quotations on pages 134 ff. may come direct from the French of Du Bartas.

chaotic Du Bartas material takes on exquisitely delicate artistic form under the shaping hand of Milton.

Milton	Du Bartas
Before their eyes in sudden view appear	The first World yet was a most formless Form,
The secrets of the hoary deep, a dark	A *confus'd heap*, a *Chaos* most deform,
Illimitable ocean, without bound,	A Gulf of Gulfs . . .
Without dimension; *where length, breadth, and highth,*	. . . *where all difference lackt:*
And time, and place, are lost; where eldest Night	*Where* th' Elements lay jumbled all together,
And *Chaos*, ancestors of Nature, hold	*Where hot and cold were jarring each with either;-*
Eternal *anarchy*, amidst the noise	The blunt with sharp, the *dank* against
Of *endless wars*, and *by confusion* stand.	the *drie*;
For *Hot, Cold, Moist*, and *Dry, four champions fierce,*	The hard with soft . . .
Strive here for mastery, and *to battle* bring	. . . and while *this brawl did last*. . . . .
	. . . .
	DB, 3 rt
Their embryon atoms; they around the flag	Earth, Aire, and Fire, were with Water mixt;
Of each his faction, in their several clans,	. . . .
Light-armed or heavy, sharp, smooth, swift, or slow,	A Heav'n un-hangd, . . .
Swarm populous, unnumbered as the sands. ii, 890 ff.	. . . .
	Where *in confusion, reigned* such *debate*. 3 rc

Those whose effects doe wholly contradict,
Longer and stronger *strive in their Conflict,*
The hot-dry fire to cold-moist Water turns not.

. . . .

With tooth and nail as *deadly foes they fight.*

. . . .

And *so in combat*.   DB, 11 rb

I saw *when* at *his word* the formless mass,	For yet, th' immortall, mighty Thunder-darter,
This World's material mould, came to a *heap*:	. . . *unto each his quarter* Had not *assigned*. DB, 3 rc

Confusion heard his voice, and wild uproar
Stood ruled, stood vast infinitude confined;
Till at his second bidding Darkness fled,
Light shone, and order from disorder sprung.
Swift to their several quarters hasted then
The cumbrous elements — earth, flood, air, fire;
And this ethereal quintessence of heaven
Flew upward, spirited with various forms,
That rolled orbicular, and *turned to stars.*   iii, 708 ff.

When the Mouth Divine
Op'ned (to each his proper place t' assigne)
Fire flew to Fire, Water to Water slid,
Aire clung to Aire, and Earth with Earth abid.
Earth, as the Lees, and heavy drosse of All
(After his kinde) did to the bottome fall.

. . . nimble *Fire*
Did . . . aspire

Unto *the top* . . .
. . . *mounted in sparks* [stars]. DB, 11 rb

Book III

In Book iii one finds a less obvious but very important influence of Du Bartas on *Paradise Lost*. The main objective of *Paradise Lost*, if we may trust Milton himself rather than the fancies of many commentators, is "to justify the ways of God to men." The modern interpreter prefers to think of this in some such terms as the reconciliation of the individual to the conditions of human existence. But the first few lines of the poem reveal what Milton means. The chief rational basis on which Milton grounds this justification is Man's free will, his original power to choose as he prefers. Free will is the causeway, to borrow a Miltonic figure, over which he passes to his objective, the justification. It is the pivotal point of the proof. This matter of free will runs as a main theme through the entire twelve books in regard to the Fall both of the angels and of man. But the main discussion occurs in elaborate development in Book iii. The connection between Milton and Du Bartas as to free will must therefore be considered at this point. It will of course occur to the reader that Milton may have got his material from various and sundry sources. He could have consulted Chaucer's *Troilus*. Or he might have gone where Chaucer is supposed to have gone, to Boëthius, or to the various other sources already indicated in this study.[1] That general compendium of knowledge, *The Mirrour of the World*, has an admirable discussion of free will. But whatever his other sources may have been, Milton certainly consulted Du Bartas. Du Bartas, like Milton, made the free-will argument the main column in the framework of the justification.[2] No single discussion of free will accessible to Milton helps to explain more adequately Milton's development of this theme in Book iii, or better illustrates his use of it throughout the poem.

A comparison of the main elaborate development of the theme in Milton and in Du Bartas shows that Milton may have actually studied and used the Du Bartas passage in detail. Du Bartas plunges us into the argument immediately after Adam and Eve have eaten the fruit. Milton gives us the argument in the words of God himself immediately before the entrance of Satan into Eden. It occupies a hundred and odd lines in Du Bartas;[3] it occupies thirty-eight lines (96 ff.) in the first of the developed discussions of Milton in Book iii of *Paradise Lost*. Sometimes the similarity between the two amounts to actual identity of phrase: as, in Du Bartas "God arms thee with" it; in Milton, "man with Freewill armed."

It is especially in regard to the use of the free-will theme in connection with the entire plan of salvation underlying the *Paradise Lost* that one is struck with Milton's relation to the free-will material of Du Bartas. All the steps of any importance in the plan by which man passes from his original state of innocence in Paradise

1. P. 20, note 8.
2. Du Bartas, 93; see the card index of Harvard College Library for the sources from which Milton *could* have got his ideas on free will.
3. P. 93.

to his condition on earth and finally to Heaven are in the *Paradise Lost* connected with the theory of free will. The same is true of Du Bartas. Du Bartas like Milton insists that God "our voluntary service requires not our necessitated." [1] There would be no real virtue, he says, in that kind of obedience which is forced:

> But free t' obey his sacred goodness still,
> Freely to follow him, and do his hest,
> *Not Philtre — charm'd nor by Busiris prest.*   DB, 93 rt

Both Milton and Du Bartas use the free-will argument as the means by which they reach a conclusion which probably appealed to both poets as the most final of the justifications of God to Man: to wit, that man's state after leaving Paradise is in fact preferable to his original state of innocence. The appreciative æsthetic critics of Milton have made much of this development of thought, stressing the larger and freer side of Milton in connection with his development of the idea. This is just, but Milton deserves credit for his development of the idea rather than for its conception. Du Bartas had been there before him; as indeed had many others.[2]

> Upon the Cross, Sin, Satan, Death and Hell;
> Making thee blessed more since thine offence
> Than in thy primer happy innocence.   DB, 93 rc

One other matter, a small one but exceedingly striking, remains to be mentioned before leaving Book iii. This book contains the only instance in which an entire line has passed bodily over from Sylvester to *Paradise Lost.*

> Immutable, Immortal, Infinite,

line 373 of Book iii, is line 45 of *The Divine Weekes.*[3]

---

1. *P.L.*, v, 530–531.
2. See above, p. 22, note 10.
3. See also Candy, *Notes and Queries*, CLVIII (1930), 93 ff.

Book IV

The magnificent Satan of Books i and ii of *Paradise Lost* shows
no signs of the influence of Du Bartas. One has not, however, gone
forward ten lines in Book iv before one meets the influence of Du
Bartas in the conception of the character of Satan. Ashton [1] has
already called attention to some of the more obvious resemblances
between the treatment of Satan in Milton and Du Bartas, arriving, however, at the conclusion: "*Le motif s'offrait naturellement à
l'esprit; L'idée que Satan pénètre comme un voleur dans le Paradis
n'a rien que d'assez banal; "La carrière de pleine maturité de Milton
est bien indépendante des influences que nous avons admises en ce
qui concerne ses œuvres de jeunesse.*" [2] Well may Ashton be con-
servative in his judgments in regard to a matter so miscellaneous
and widespread as the treatment of Satan in the Middle Ages and
the Renaissance.

But when one considers the details gathered by Aşhton, plus
numerous others presently to be cited, — the extraordinary similarity of the phrasing, and the still more extraordinary fineness of
the degree of similarity in subtle shades of thought, — it is impossible to escape the conclusion that Milton was definitely affected
by Du Bartas.

Satan's state of mind as he enters Eden is emphasized, and to a
very detailed degree, in *Paradise Lost*: — "now first inflamed with
rage"; "Now rolling, boils in his tumultuous breast"; "Horror and
doubt distract his troubled thought"; "Now conscience wakes
despair"; "Wakes the bitter memory of what he was"; "Each
passion dimmed his face, . . . *Ire, envy*, and *despair*, Which marred
his borrowed visage"; "his gestures fierce and mad demeanour";
"But the hot hell that in him burns, Though in mid Heaven."

1. *Du Bartas en Angleterre*, Paris, 1908, pp. 301 ff.
2. The same, pp. 302, 305.

Observe the same stuff in raw form in Du Bartas as descriptive of the state of mind of Satan when he enters Eden:

> Feels a pestiferous busie swarming nest
>
> .   .   .   .
> Pinching his entrails with ten thousand tongues,
> His coursed soule still most extreamely *racking*.
>
> .   .   .   .   .
> But above all, *Hate*, *Pride* and *Envious spight*
> His hellish life do torture day and night.
>
> Spurs on his course, his *rage* redoubling still   DB, 90 lt

The prime motive [1] that brings all these boiling passions to a head and makes them burst is the same in both poets: man's resemblance to his maker, God. The language is entirely too similar to be accidental. Although Milton's Satan is tempted to relent as he looks and "could love; so lively *shines in them divine resemblance*," [2] this resemblance of Adam to his maker later becomes the chief motivating force for his revenge on God; it is this mainly which urges him on:

> I reck not, so it [revenge] light well aim'd,
> Since higher I fall short, on him who next
> Provokes my Envy, this new favourite
> Of Heaven, this man of clay, son of despite,
> Whom, us the more to spite, his Maker raised
> From dust: spite then with spite is best repaid.   ix, 173 ff.

Du Bartas puts it less gracefully, but he expresses the same idea in similar language:

> And th' Envious heart-break to see (yet) *to shine*
> In *Adam's face God's image all divine*,
> Which he had lost; and that Man might achieve
> The glorious bliss his Pride did him deprive.
>
> Spurs-on his course, his rage redoubling still.   DB, 90 lt

---

1. Fletcher, *Milton's Rabbinical Readings*, pp. 184, 185, suggests that it is his jealousy of Adam's sexual happiness with Eve which is the prime motive; it is only one of many motives.   2. P.L., iv, 364.

In *Paradise Lost* Satan enters: "as when a prowling wolf"; "or as a *thief*"; "as when a ship, by skillful steer'sman wrought Nigh river's mouth"; as an "*Admiral*." In Du Bartas he enters: "Much like (therefore) some *thief*"; "The Dragon then, Man's fortress to surprise, Follows some *captain's* martial policies."[1] In both Milton and Du Bartas Satan tries the different animals before deciding on the serpent. In *Paradise Lost*:

> Down he alights among the sportful herd
> ... *himself now one* —
>
> *A lion now* he stalks. . . .
> *Then as a tiger*."   iv, 396–403

In Du Bartas:

> Thinks *now the beauty* of an Horse to borrow;
> Anon to creep into a Heifer's side:
> *Then in a Cock*, or in a Dog to hide.   DB, 90 rt

In both poets we find the same attempt to give the impression of a hidden danger ready at any moment to pounce upon its prey. In *Paradise Lost*:

> ... As one who *chose his ground*,
> Whence rushing he might surest seize them both.   iv, 406–407

In Du Bartas:

> Much like — some thief that . . .
> .   .   .   .   .   .
> ... neer the King's high-way
> Himself doth *ambush* in a bushy Thorn.   DB, 90 lb

In both Milton and Du Bartas, once the serpent is "inhabited" by Satan, there arises the difficulty of explaining God's condemnation of the serpent. Both poets attempt an explanation, and both admit that they are baffled and so leave the matter unexplained. In *Paradise Lost*:

---

1. Du Bartas, 91.

The Fiend
Mere serpent in appearance.   ix, 412–413

To judgment he proceeded on the accused
Serpent, though brute, unable to transfer
The guilt on him who made him *instrument*
Of mischief, and polluted from the end
Of his creation; justly then accursed,
As vitiated in nature.   More to know
Concerned not Man.   x, 161 ff.

Although, only eighty-nine lines before, Christ has said, "Conviction to the Serpent none belongs," [1] God here proceeds to pass judgment on the serpent, "though in mysterious terms." [2] Compare Du Bartas:

No very Serpent, but a Serpent's shape.   DB, 90 rc

Yet tis a doubt whether the Divell did
Governe the Dragon. . . .

.   .   .   .

Locally absent, present by effect.

Or whether for a time he did abide
Within the doubling Serpent's damask hide.

But this stands sure, how-ever else it went,
The old Serpent serv'd as Satan's *instrument.*

But (to conclude) I think 't was no conceipt,
No feined Idoll . . .

.   .   .   .

But the self Serpent.

Yet 'tis doubt whether the Divell did
Govern the Dragon.   DB, 91 lc

In both Milton and Du Bartas Satan assails Eve "through the organs of her fancy."   In *Paradise Lost*:

1. *P.L.*, x, 84.
2. The same, x, 173.

> Him there they found
> Squat like a toad, close at the ear of Eve,
> *Assaying by his devilish art to reach*
> The *organs of her fancy*, and with *them forge*
> Illusions as he list, phantasms and *dreams*.   iv, 799 ff.

In Du Bartas:

> Sometimes me seems, troubling Eve's spirit, the Fiend,
> *Made her his speaking fancy apprehend.*
> For . . .
>
> .   .   .   .
>
> The evill angels slide too easily
> As subtle Spirits int' our *fantasie*.   DB, 90 lc

In both poets Satan, in his initial approach to Eve, is said to be extremely eloquent, and the terms in which they both describe this eloquence are very similar. In both his power of language is a *mystery* to be interpreted similarly:

> With serpent-tongue
> Organic, or *impulse of vocal air*,
> His fraudulent temptation thus began.   ix, 529 ff.

This is clarified as to its exact meaning by the following illuminating passage from Du Bartas:

> Yet 'tis a doubt whether the Divell did
> Governe the Dragon, not there selfly hid,
> To . . . his tongue direct,
> *Locally absent, present by effect:*
> *As when the sweet strings of a Lute we strike,*
> *Another lute laid neer it, sounds the like.*   DB, 91 lc

In Milton the Serpent's eloquence is emphasized by two extraordinary literary touches: "As when of old some *orator* renowned";[1] "So *glozed* the tempter and his proem tuned."[2] Both find their anticipation in Du Bartas:

> This self-dumb Creature *glozing* Rhetorike
> With bashfull shame great *Orators* would strike.   DB, 91 lb

---

1. *P.L.*, ix, 670.   2. The same, ix, 549.

In both poets the culminating point of this rhetorical gift is shown in the extraordinary epithets of flattery addressed to Eve. Note their variety and their similarity. In Milton: "Sovran mistress"; "Fairest resemblance to thy Maker fair"; "A Goddess among Gods"; "Empress of this fair world"; "resplendent Eve"; "Sovern of creatures"; "Universal Dame"; "Empress"; "Queen of the Universe"; "Goddess humane." In Du Bartas: "Eve, second honour of this Universe"; "Fair"; "O Worlds rare glory." [1]

It is in Book iv of *Paradise Lost* also that one runs across perhaps the favorite epic formula of Du Bartas. Time and again when handling a purely conjectural subject, he resorts to the formula, "whether . . . or." It is almost as pronounced a mannerism in Du Bartas as Milton's "when" in the introductory formulæ for his similes. But the striking thing about the use of this formula in both poets is that it is employed in both as the *formula of scientific doubt*. Milton first uses it when balancing in his own mind the truth of the Ptolemaic and the Copernican system:

Whether the prime orb,
Incredible how swift, had thither rolled
Diurnal, *or* this less volubil Earth,
By shorter flight to the east, had left him there.   iv, 592 ff.

Whether heaven move *or* Earth,
Imports not, if thou reckon right.
                              viii, 70–71

But *whether* thus these things, *or whether* not —
Whether the sun, predominant in heaven,

Whether God's spirit moving upon the Ball
Of bubbling Waters, which yet covered All. . . .

Whether, when God the mingled Lump dispackt. . . .

.   .   .   .

Whether about the vast confused Crowd
Or *whether* [2] else some other Lamp he kindled.   DB, 5 lt

---

1. Du Bartas, 91, 92.
2. See for other instances Du Bartas, 6, 13, 18 ff.

Rise on the Earth, *or* Earth rise on the
    sun;
He from the east his flaming road
    begin,
Or she from west her silent course
    advance.   viii, 159 ff.

It is in Book iv also that Du Bartas has contributed to one of
Milton's most exquisite passages both as to thought and as to expression. Eve, as she looks up at the firmament with Adam, inquires of him why all the constellations continue to shine while he
and she are asleep:

But wherefore all night long *shine* these? for whom
This glorious sight, when sleep hath shut all eyes?
To whom our general ancestor replied:

.   .   .   .

Those have their course to finish round the Earth . . .

.   .   .   .

Ministering light prepared, they set and rise;
Lest total Darkness should by night regain
Her old possession, and extinguish life
In nature and in all things; which *these soft fires*
Not only enlighten, but with kindly heat
Of various influence foment and warm,
Temper or nourish, or in part *shed down*
Their stellar virtue on all *kinds that grow* . . .
These . . .
Shine not in vain.   iv, 657 ff.

If the similarities of thought and expression are noted in the Du
Bartas passage below it will be rather difficult to doubt its direct
influence:

I'l ne'r beleeve that the Arch-Architect,
With all *these Fires* the Heav'nly Arches deckt
Onely for Shew, and with these glistring shields
T' amaze poor Shepheards watching in the fields,
I'l ne'r beleeve that the *least flower* that pranks

.   .   .   .

Hath some *peculiar virtue* of its own;
And that the glorious Stars of Heav'n have *none* [stellar virtue]
But shine in vain, and have no charge precise,
But to be walking in Heav'n's Galleries.   DB, 35 lt

It is in Book iv also that Milton introduces his epithalamium in connection with the marriage of Adam and Eve (750 ff.). Du Bartas introduces his epithalamium in the same connection. Milton did not need the aid of Du Bartas; accessible marriage hymns both in classical and in Renaissance literature abounded. It is noteworthy, however, that Milton's emphasis on chastity in this context may after all be simply a commonplace or a literary convention, for Du Bartas is just as emphatic:

Source of all *joys*. . . .

O chastest friendship!   DB, 57 rb

By thee, we quench the wild and wanton Fires.

.   .   .   .

And taught by thee a love more firm and fitter.   DB, 58 lt

This is the thought of Milton but not his language, which proves to be, though not dissimilar in all respects, decidedly superior:

Hail, wedded love, mysterious law, true *source*
Of human offspring.

.   .   .   .

By thee adulterous lust was driven from men.

.   .   .   .

Perpetual *fountain of* domestic *sweets*.   iv, 750 ff.

The comment of the two poets, that God has commanded sexual relations, is placed by both outside the epithalamium proper, — just before it in *Paradise Lost*:

What God *declares*
Pure, and *commands* to *some*, leaves free to all —   iv, 746–747

long after it in Du Bartas:[1]

> By *God* and *Nature* . . .
> Rather *commanded then allowed*, and grac't
> In their sweet fruits.   DB, 155 lc

Saurat stresses this attitude towards marriage as indicative of Milton's modernity.[2]

Book V

Milton's indebtedness to Du Bartas in Book v is heavy. In the exact method by which Satan persuades Eve to take the fruit Du Bartas anticipates Milton's Satan:

> Here . . . *fair* angelic Eve,
>
> .   .   .   .   .   .
>
> Taste this, and be henceforth among the gods
> Thyself a goddess.   v, 74 ff.

The same subject is continued in Book ix:

> Why then was this forbid?   Why but to awe
> Why but to keep ye low and ignorant,
> His worshippers?   He knows that in the day
> Ye eat therof, *your eyes that seem so clear*,
> Yet *are but dim*, shall perfectly be then
> Opened and cleared.   ix, 703 ff.

> What hinders then,
> To *reach* and feed at once both body and mind?   ix, 778–779

> Goddess humane, *reach* then and freely taste.   ix, 732

Milton's poetry is vastly better, of course, but his relation to Du Bartas is none the less clear:

> Eve, *Second honour of this Universe*!
> Is't true, I pray, that jealous God, perverse,
> Forbids, quoth he, both you and all your race
> All the fair Fruits . . .?   DB, 91 rb

---

1. See also Du Bartas, 58 l.
2. *Milton, Man and Thinker*, p. 159.

No, *fair*, quoth he, beleeve not, that the care
God hath, Mankinde from spoyling death to spare,
Makes him forbid you . . .

.　.　.　.　.　.　.　.　.　.

Sith the suspected vertue of This Tree
Shall soon disperse the *cloud of Idiocy*,
Which *dims your eyes*; and further, make you seem
Excelling us, even equal Gods to him.
O Worlds rare glory! *reach* thy happy hand,
Reach, reach, I say.　　　　　　　　　　　DB, 92 lt

It is in Book v also that we meet one of those splendid hymns of praise to the Creator, found elsewhere in *Paradise Lost*, now recited by Adam or Eve or angels, now by Milton himself.[1] Imbedded as they are in the epic, these are no conventional hymns but rather beautiful aspirations like Coleridge's *Hymn before Sunrise in the Valley of Chamouni*. There is nothing greater in English hymnology.[2] Doubtless Milton was influenced by his familiarity with the great hymns to God in the Bible or with the Medieval Latin hymns. But it is certainly worth noting that about the same number of hymns to God the Creator occur in the religious epic of Du Bartas, and that they stress practically the same points and are used for the same interpretative purpose.[3] Both poets, through their hymns to God, point to the objective world in all its multitudinous detail as the chief exciting stimulus to *wonder* and *admiration*, and discourage over-curious inquiry into the "secrets of God"; they both add to this almost the same mystical interpretation of these details in such a way as to arrive at identically the same varieties of religious experience, using moreover phrases exactly similar in connection with the same matters. Many of these interpretations are used, to be sure, by other writers of

1. iii, 702 ff.; iv, 674 ff.; v, 153 ff.; vii, 602 ff.; viii, 15 ff., 66 ff., 273 ff.
2. See Louise Lanham, *Hymnic Elements in Milton's Poetry*, MS. dissertation, University of North Carolina, 1927.
3. Du Bartas, 2, 27, 40, 49, 53, 60, 117.

hymns, here and there, but not all of them by any one writer with whom Milton has been shown to be familiar. Add to this the fact that both poets through the treatment of Nature in detail in the hymns finally arrive at their philosophical interpretation of the universe and even at the same final definition of the Prime Wisdom, and it is reasonable to infer some definite use by Milton of the *Divine Weekes*.

Neither poet seems to tire of repeating the variations which appear in their hymns, best known perhaps in Milton:

Milton	Du Bartas
For heaven Is as the *Book* of God before thee set, Wherein to read his wondrous *works*. viii, 66 ff.	The World's a *Book* in Folio, printed all With God's great *Works* in letters Capitall. DB, 2 rt
These are thy glorious works, Parent of good, Almighty! thine *this universal frame*, Thus wondrous fair: thyself how wondrous then! . . . *dimly* seen In these thy lowest works. v, 153 ff.	God, of himself, incapable to sense, In's Works reveals him t'our intelligence. DB, 2 rc
For wonderful indeed are all his works, Pleasant to know, and worthiest to be all Had in remembrance always with delight. iii, 702 ff.	I love to look on God; but, in this Robe Of his great Works, *this Universall Globe*. DB, 2 rc
When I behold *this goodly frame*, this World. viii, 15	As well our wits as our weak eyes to bring . . . *In't admiration*, that men . . . Praising his works, might praise their Maker more. DB, 40 rt
From Man or Angel *the great Architect* Did wisely to conceal, and not divulge His secrets, to be scanned by them who ought Rather *admire*. viii, 72 ff.	So th' *Architect* (whose glorious Workmanships My cloudy Muse doth but too much eclipse). DB, 60 lt

Therefore by *Faith's* pure rayes il-
lumined,
The sacred Pandects I desire to read,
And, God the better to behold,

Heaven is for thee too high   behold
To know what passes there; *be lowly* Th' Orb from his Birth.   DB, 3 lc
   wise.   viii, 172–173 *Be sober wise*: so, bound thy frail
desire:
And what thou canst not comprehend,
   admire.   DB, 161 lc

Perhaps the most deeply tragic thought that comes to Adam
when he realizes that he must leave Eden is connected with the
idea that he shall no longer be able to read even dimly in the Book
of God's works. And perhaps the most stimulating thought which
Michael leaves with Adam is that this is one book which he can
always read everywhere:

> In yonder nether world where shall I seek
> His bright appearances, or footstep trace?   xi, 328–329

The answer is,

> Yet doubt not but in valley and in plain
> God is, as here, and will be found alike
> Present, and of his presence many a sign
> Still following thee.   xi, 349 ff.

This is, of course, a stroke of Milton's genius; but Du Bartas is
visible in the background, much as one may be disinclined to believe it. Of Adam in Eden Du Bartas says:

> For, yer his Fall, which way so e'er he rowl'd,
> His wondering eyes, God everywhere behold;
> In Heav'n, in Earth, in Ocean, and in Aire,
> He sees, and feels, and findes him everywhere.   DB, 96 rt

This desire to trace God's footsteps, "to find him everywhere,"
underlies the entire body of the *Divine Weekes*. Du Bartas, indeed, expressly says that it is one of the main motives of his
works.

Thus the hymnic elements in Milton and Du Bartas are not only remarkably alike but lead up to the same philosophic end, — *wonder* and *admiration* in beholding the visible garment of God, the World. Finally, an examination of the approaches of Milton and Du Bartas to God and Nature yields some highly significant results. Both poets lay an amazing emphasis on the right of Man to inquire objectively into God and Nature, terms which Du Bartas sometimes uses synonymously. Both insist repeatedly that such inquiry leads to worship and admiration of God. Both deny the right of Man to push these inquiries to the point of ferreting out God's mysteries.

The treatment of the Book of God's works is advanced by Greenlaw among other evidences of Milton's debt to Spenser.[1] Of late an interest in the Book of God's works is regarded apparently as an indication of the influence of the Newtonian physics in eighteenth-century English poetry.[2] The idea, however, was a commonplace even in the Middle Ages. That popular *L'Image du Monde* of Gossouin in 1245 expresses it in a fashion not essentially different from that of the Renaissance:[3]

Si penserent bien en leur sens, comme gent qui espoient de noble pourpens, que ja connoissance n'avroient ne de Dieu, ne de sa poissance, se il n'enqueroient avant en ses euvres, tant comme il en pourroient savoir. Car ja bien ne connoitra l'en le mestre, se l'en ne connoist son estre avant, et ses euvres queles eles sont. Car par les euvres connoist on l'ouvrier et comment il peut estre. Et pour ce se voudrent essaier aus euvres Dieu premierement por plus legierement avoir connoissance de son pouoir et de sa vertu. Et quant plus porroient savoir de ses euvres et de ses sens, tant avroient il meilleur volenté d'amer leur createur, et meilleur pourpens, qui avoit fet si noble chose comme estoit le ciel qu'il veoient, les estoiles qui reluisoient par mi, et ses autres vertuz merveilleuses dont il le prisoient plus. Et tant comme plus le prisoient, [et] plus le servoient volentiers. Car ce estoit toute leur entention et toute leur raison de Dieu connoistre.

---

1. *The New Science and English Literature in the Seventeenth Century*, *The Johns Hopkins Alumni Magazine*, XIII (1925), 331 ff.

2. George G. Williams, *The Beginnings of Nature Poetry in the Eighteenth Century*, *Studies in Philology*, XXVII (1930), 602 ff.

3. *L'Image du Monde*, ed. Prior, 70.

Under the shelter of the text "the Heavens declare the Glory of God and the firmament showeth his Handiwork," science could pursue its investigation into the world of matter. In view of the commonplace nature of the thought, therefore, it is not of any great importance that the idea occurs in both Milton and Du Bartas. It is of importance that its use and expression in the two epics should be so similar.

Book VI

There appear to be no borrowings from Du Bartas in Book vi.

Book VII

The influence of Du Bartas upon Milton in Book vii is definite and very extensive. Perhaps nowhere else is it clearer and more unmistakable.

It is in Book vii, it will be remembered, that Milton condenses the story of the creation to which Du Bartas devotes an immense portion of *La Sepmaine*. In this process of condensation one has an opportunity to observe, as one rarely has, Milton artistically fashioning crude material into perfect forms. Take, for instance, the following unmistakably clear example of Milton's handling of material already provided in the *Divine Weekes*. From one brief sentence in Genesis, — "And God said, Let the waters under the Heavens be gathered together into one place, and let the dry land appear," — Du Bartas succeeded in developing a description wonderful in its multiplicity of detail and extremely effective. Parts of it affected Milton most profoundly:

> All those steep *Mountains*, whose high horned tops
> The misty cloak of wandring *Clouds* enwraps,
> *Under first Waters their crump shoulders hid,*
> And all the Earth, as a dull Pond abid,
> Untill th' all-Monarch's bounteous Majesty
>
> .   .   .   .

Commanding Neptune straight to marshall forth
His Floods apart.

. . . .

Ev'n so the Sea, to 't self it self betook,
Mount after Mount, Field after Field forsook;

. . . .

Her Waters, that from ev'ry side did run.   DB, 21 lr

Lo, thus the weighty Water did ere-while
With winding turns make all this World an Ile,
For, *like as moulten Lead being poured forth
Upon a levell plat of sand or earth,
In many fashions mazeth to and fro;*

. . . .

Here doth divide itselfe, there meets again;

. . . .

Almost, in th' instant, ev'ry form doth form:
God pour'd the Waters on the fruitfull Ground
In sundry figures;   DB, 22 lc

. . . .

   and down the *water leaps*
On every side; it foams, it *roars*, it *rushes*,
And through the steep and stony hils it gushes,
Making *a thousand brooks; whereof, when one
Perceives his fellow striving to be gone,
Hasting his course, he him accompanies;*
After, another and another *hies*,
All in one race.   DB, 22 rc

The number of details in this description which have left their in-
delible impression on Milton is astonishing. The *curious patterns*
made by the waters as they move about, the *drops separating and
collecting* when poured out on a flat surface, especially the *haste* of
the waters small and large as they get together, and their *eagerness*
both in obeying the "command" and in "racing" to meet each
other, are all to be found in Milton's description:

> Be gathered now ye Waters under heaven,
> Into one place, and let dry land appear.
> Immediately the *Mountains huge* appear

Emergent, and *their broad bare backs upheave*
Into the clouds.

.   .   .   .

                              So low
Down sunk a hollow bottom, broad and deep,
Capacious bed of waters; thither they
Hasted with glad precipitance, uprolled,
As *drops on dust conglobing from the dry*;
Part rise in crystal wall, or ridge direct,
For haste; such flight the great command impressed
On the swift floods. *As armies at the call
Of Trumpet . . .*
Troop to their standard, so *the watery throng*,
Wave rolling after wave, . . .
. . . *with torrent rapture*, if through plain,
Soft-ebbing; nor withstood them rock or hill,
But they, . . .
With serpent error wandering, found thir way,
And on the washy ooze deep channels wore.   vii, 283 ff.

When one turns back to the beginning of Book vii and proceeds to examine it throughout, one will observe that Milton gets from Du Bartas many suggestions as to the details of the creation on each of the six days, and, in addition, suggestions as to the method of presenting these details.

Book vii opens with a variation of the Urania motive highly suggestive of the Urania motives scattered through *The Divine Weekes*. But that is of little importance when compared with other connections between the two works. In Du Bartas, Adam and Seth occupy a relation exactly analogous to the tutorial [1] relation of Raphael and Adam in *Paradise Lost*:

Old Seth, saith Heber, Adam's Scholar yerst
Who was the Scholler of his Maker first,
Having attain'd to know the course and sites,
Th' aspect and greatness of Heav'ns glistering lights.
                              DB, 136 lt

---

1. M. W. Bundy, *Milton's View of Education in Paradise Lost, Journal of English and Germanic Philology*, xxi (1922), 127 ff. See also, as to Adam's thirst for knowledge, Bruce, *The Nation*, New York, xcvii (1913), 33.

The very matter which Adam and Seth begin to discuss, the very spirit in which they discuss it, and the language employed, are similar enough to show the relation between the two poets. And if these similarities are not sufficient to convince the most skeptical, add to them the unquenchable Renaissance thirst for knowledge with which these two — Adam in *Paradise Lost*, Seth in Du Bartas — are possessed about the same matters. In *Paradise Lost* we have:

> . . . Adam . . .
>
> .   .   .   .
>
> Led on . . . with desire to know
> . . . *how this World*
> Of Heaven and Earth *conspicuous first began*;
> *When, and whereof created; for what cause;*
>
> .   .   .   .
>
> . . . as one *whòse drouth*
> Yet scarce allayed still eyes the current stream,
> Whose liquid murmur heard new thirst excites.   vii, 59 ff.

In Du Bartas:

> Him he instructeth in the wayes of Veritie,
>
> .   .   .   .
>
> To *know Heav'ns course*, and *how their constant swaies*
> *Divide the year* in months, the months in dayes.
>
> .   .   .   .
>
> No sooner he his lessons can commence,
> But Seth hath hit the White of his intents.
>
> .   .   .   .
>
> The *more he knows, the more he craves*; as fuell
> Kils not a fire, but *kindles* it more cruel.
>
>   DB, 108 lm

At this juncture asks Seth, "*how* the Lord the Heav'ns about *this all* did bow; *what things* have hot, *and what* have cold effect and *how* my life and manners to direct." [1] Many of the details in what Adam says to Seth are similar to those in Raphael's discourse to

1. Du Bartas, 108.

Adam. Both dialogues concern the creation of the world and the events of the several days. In this particular passage of Du Bartas the account of the creation is much more condensed than Raphael's account to Adam in *Paradise Lost*. Elsewhere in Du Bartas the account is much more fully elaborated.[1] Before proceeding, however, to consider the relation of the details of Book vii to those of Du Bartas, it is well to observe the strikingly similar method in which the details of Old Testament history are revealed to Adam in *Paradise Lost*, and to Seth in Du Bartas, as future events. This is done in *Paradise Lost* not by Raphael but by a less sociable and intimate instructor, Michael,[2] in Books xi and xii. In Book xi the details are presented to Adam in the form of a vision. In the same set of instructions, which Adam is giving to Seth [3] in Du Bartas, Adam is also forced to have recourse to a vision, and many of the episodes are exactly the same that are thus recounted by Milton. In this particular part of his work Du Bartas presents his material in a much less elaborate form than Milton. In the following books, however, — such as The Ark, Babalon, The Colonies, The Columnes, The Fathers, — his material is far more elaborately presented than Milton's. The actual use which Milton made of these books of Du Bartas will be studied later. At this point, however, must be noticed Milton's use of the end of the dialogue between Adam and Seth in Du Bartas. No other passage illustrates more strikingly how Milton got from this dialogue an extremely effective method of presenting the significant parts of Old Testament history as an organic portion of his plan for the justification of the ways of God to Man. Throughout Michael's narrative of the

1. For example, in the Books of Du Bartas entitled *The First Day of the First Week* and the other days of this first week, which will now be taken up in detail as to their direct relation to the remainder of Book vii of *Paradise Lost*.

2. For Michael and the visions of Adam, see E. C. Baldwin, *Paradise Lost and the Apocalypse of Moses, Journal of English and Germanic Philology*, xxiv (1925), 383–386.

3. Du Bartas, 108 rt.

different epochs of history connected with Adam's descendants, Adam is made with dramatic effectiveness to cry out in his agony at the sight of the sins and sufferings of his future children. Exactly so in Du Bartas, and for the same reason. These are the exclamations of Adam at the sight of the calamities as they befall his descendants:

> O sight
> Of terror, foul and ugly to behold!
> Horrid to think, how horrible to feel!   xi, 463
>
> O miserable Mankind!   xi, 500
>
> O pity and shame!   xi, 629
>
> O visions ill foreseen!   Better had I
> Lived ignorant of future!   xi, 763–764
>
> O execrable son!   xii, 64

Compare, in Du Bartas, the laments of Adam after he has related similar matters of the future to Seth, — and in a vision likewise, which, as in *Paradise Lost*, leaves him "almost dead for wo." [1]

> Alas! so many Nephews lose I here.
> .   .   .   .
> O Children whither fly you?
> .   .   .   .
> O Son-lesse Father!   O too fruitfull hanches!
> O wretched root!   O hurtfull, hateful branches.
> .   .   .   .
> O Flesh! O Bloud! Here, sorrow stopt the door
> Of his sad voyce; and, almost dead for wo . . .   DB, 109 rb

Many are the details which Milton uses in his description during the rest of Book vii, which he could or did get from Du Bartas. But of that the reader may judge for himself as they are now presented in detail. There is nothing particularly startling about the fact that Milton prefaces his description of the creation in Book vii with the remark, "Immediate are the acts of God," [2] and that Du

---

1. Du Bartas, 109 rb.   2. *P.L.*, vii, 176.

Bartas says "The Word and Deed, all in an instant wrought." [1] In theological literature, before and after Milton, this is a platitude.[2] When, however, we note that Milton also prefaces this description with a conception of a God who mathematically lays out the plans for this universal scheme, and that Du Bartas does the same, that is another matter.

> He took the golden compasses, prepared
> In God's eternal store, to circumscribe
> This Universe, and all created things.
> One foot he centred, and the other turned
> Round through the vast profundity obscure,
> And said, "Thus far extend, thus far thy bounds,
> This be thy just circumference, O World." vii, 225 ff.

The idea lies in the mind of both the God of Du Bartas and of Milton and is in both mathematically and Platonically conceived. In Du Bartas:

> But if (my Son) this superficiall gloze
> Suffice the not; then may we thus suppose,
> That as before th' All-working Word alone
> Made Nothing be All's womb and Embryon,
> Th' eternall Plot, th' "Idea" fore-conceiv'd,
> The wondrous Form of all that Form receiv'd,
> *Did in the Work-mans spirit divinely lie;*
> And, yer it was, the World was wondrously; DB, 140 rb

> Th' Eternall Trine-One, spreading even the Tent
> Of th' All enlightning glorious Firmament,
> Fill'd it with figures; and in various Marks
> There pourtray'd Tables of his future Works.
> . . . .
> There's nothing precious in Sea, Earth, or Aire,
> But hath in Heav'n some like resemblance faire.
> Yea, even our Crowns, Darts, Lances, Skeyns, and Scales,
> Are all but Copies of Heav'ns Principals;
> And sacred *patterns* which to serve all Ages,
> Th' Almighty printed on Heav'ns ample stages. DB, 141 lt

---

1. Du Bartas, 551.

2. See p. 19, note 5, above. Du Bartas says elsewhere that creation came "not all at once."

It is at the very end of the creation that Milton adds the effect of
neo-Platonism which we observe in Du Bartas:

> How it showed
> In prospect from his throne, how good, how fair,
> Answering his great Idea.   vii, 555–557

Du Bartas's suggestion that God had a mathematical as well as
Platonic plan before he began his created world, comes at the end
of his elaborate discussion of the mathematical sciences as handed
down by Heber to the descendants of Adam. Further suggestions
of this neo-Platonic conception of the creation Milton throws in as
to both plants and animals: [1]

> And each
> Plant of the field, which ere it was in the Earth
> God made.   vii, 334 ff.

> Innumerous living creatures, perfect forms.   vii, 455

As the conception of chaos in Book vii [2] has already been noticed
in the two poets in connection with the chaos of Book ii, the discussion may now proceed at once to the amazing number of details
in Milton's description of the work of the six days which he could
have got, if he had seen fit, from Du Bartas. That he got them all
from Du Bartas is not necessarily to be assumed, for many of them
are conventional, and might have been acquired by Milton from
various and sundry sources, such as Medieval or Renaissance bes-
tiaries, lapidaries, botanies, or from Pliny's *Natural History*. Still,
in view of the unquestionable borrowing on a large scale in regard
to other matters of the creation, the following exactly similar details in the two works lead one to conclude that the use of Du
Bartas here is very, very great.

1. Fletcher, *Milton's Rabbinical Readings*, pp. 122 ff., 156 ff.
2. vii, 233 ff.

It is noticeable that what Du Bartas leaves as an open question, — one of the possibilities of the exact method of creating the
Sun, — Milton apparently adopts:[1]

> Whether, when God the mingled Lump dispackt,
> From Fiery Element did Light extract:
> Whether about the vast confused Crowd
> For twice six-hours he spread a *shining Cloud.*
>
> .   .   .   .
>
> *God's eldest Daughter.*   DB, 5 rt

> 'Let ther be light,' said God; and forthwith light
> Ethereal, *first of things*, . . .
> Sprung from the Deep, and from her native east
> To journey through the aery gloom began,
> Sphered in a *radiant cloud, for yet the sun
> Was not*; she in a *cloudy* tabernacle
> Sojourned the while.   vii, 243 ff.

Following this in Milton comes the statement that the World was
not yet born:

> *The Earth was formed,* but in the *womb* as yet
> Of waters, *embryon* immature, involved,
> Appeared not.   vii, 276 ff.

Compare Du Bartas:

> That as before th' All-working Word alone
> Made Nothing be All's *womb and Embryon,*
> Th' eternall Plot, th' Idea fore-conceiv'd,
> The wondrous *form* of all that Form receiv'd,
> *Did* in the Work-man's spirit divinely *lie.*   DB, 140 rb

> This was not then the World: 'twas but the Matter,
> The *Nurcery* whence it should issue after;
> Or rather, the *Embryon,* that within a Weeke
> Was to be born.   DB, 3 rb

There follows in Milton the further description of light as
gathered in the Sun, biggest of "lightsome bodies." The enthusi-

---

1. See Robbins, *The Hexaemeral Literature*, p. 80; Fletcher, *Milton's Rabbinical Readings*, p. 149.

asm with which Du Bartas greets the Sun, and the epithets [1] which he showers upon this great constellation, are similar to an extraordinary degree both in importance and in elaborated description to those which Milton gives to Light and the Sun in *Paradise Lost*. Indeed, Milton is the Sun-worshipper among all the lovers of light in English poetry. It is not to be ignored that Du Bartas [2] discourses and digresses on this subject almost to the extent of Milton himself, indulging in some one hundred and odd lines which anticipate Milton in many expressions of extraordinary power and beauty. Although Milton knew and liked other poetical and prose glorifications of the Sun, is it not fair to assume that he got some of the following details from Du Bartas?

All-hail pure Lamp.	DB, 5 rc
. . . .	
Thou World's great Taper.	DB, 5 rc
Fountain . . . of Light.	DB, 35 rb
Life of the World.	DB, 35 rb
Lamp of this Universe. O teach me where I may but begin thy praise	DB, 35 rb
. . . .	
Day's glorious Eye!	DB, 35 rb
Scarce I begin to measure thy bright Face.	DB, 36 lc
. . . .	
But that fantastikly I change my Theam.	DB, 36 lc
God's eldest Daughter.	DB, 5 rc

Milton reacts to the first appearance of the newly created sun with the same unbounded enthusiasm as Du Bartas:

First in the east the glorious *lamp* was seen, Regent of day.	vii, 370–371
Great palace now of *light*. Hither, as to their *fountain*, other stars Repairing, . . .	vii, 363 ff.

---

1. Du Bartas, 35 ff.   2. The same.

In Milton immediately afterwards come the stars, —

> With thousand thousand stars, that then appeared
> *Spangling* the hemisphere.   vii, 383–384

In Du Bartas the sky at creation is

> not yet *spangled* with their fiery sparks.   DB, 3 rm

and when finally finished is:

> richly *spangled* with bright glistring-sparks.   DB, 32 lt

The details as to the different groups of created things in Milton and Du Bartas are so similar in their order as to make it difficult to doubt that Milton drew on Du Bartas. Vegetable life begins:

> *He scarce had said* when the bare Earth, till then
> Desert and bare, unsightly, unadorned . . .   vii, 313 314

Under the figure of speech of a beautiful woman decorating herself or being decorated as for an entertainment, the earth begins to take on now this, now that aspect of herbal or vegetable life. It is under the same figure of speech in Du Bartas that the same details of vegetable life are arranged. *"No sooner spoken but"* describes the suddenness with which the herb-life obeys the command of God (p. 25). Compare the *"He scarce had said"* of Milton (vii, 313).[1]

> Change, change (quoth he), O fair and firmest Globe,
> Thy mourning weed, to a green gallant Robe;
>
> .   .   .   .
>
> Cheer thy sad brows and stately garnish them
> With a rich fragrant, flow'ry Diadem;
> Lay forth thy locks and paint thee (Lady-like)
> With freshest colours on they sallow cheek.
> And let from henceforth thy abundant breasts.   DB, 25 rc

---

1. See Fletcher, *Milton's Rabbinical Readings*, pp. 158, 159, for Rashi's treatment of the earth clothed as with a garment. See also "no sooner said . . . but" in Du Bartas in connection with *immediate* creation of light.

This passage in Du Bartas is followed by the description of the trees which, "th' Airy Mountains mantle round about," [1] a figure which in Milton appears as "With high woods the hills were crowned." And the contrast of the vegetation in the valleys with that in the mountains which appears in Du Bartas as:

> The winding *rivers bordered all their banks*
> With slice-Sea Alders, and green Osiars small.   DB, 25 rb

appears thus in Milton:

> With tufts the valleys and each fountain-side,
> With *borders long the rivers.*   vii, 327–328

In Du Bartas the different trees,

> Through Hill and Plain ranged their plumed Ranks.
>   DB, 25 rb

In Milton:

> Rose, as in a dance, the stately trees.   vii, 324

Du Bartas's "amorous vine" becomes "the clustering vine" of Milton; Du Bartas's "Maiz, a Reed" becomes "the corny reed," and when Milton follows this with the phrase *"embattled* in her field" it looks very much as if he may have got the suggestion from Du Bartas's

> The Fields of Corn, as Fields of *Combat* first.   DB, 29 rb

From the animal life in Du Bartas Milton gets even more than from the vegetable. Much of the curious Miltonic lore about both plants and animals which strikes the modern reader as almost unintelligible may be explained by his selection of only a few of Du Bartas's interminable details. Of course both poets knew Pliny well, but Pliny will hardly account for some of the resemblances. Thus the Miltonic fish which

> attend
> *Moist nutriment,* or *under rocks their food*
> In jointed armor watch,   vii, 407 ff.

---

1. Du Bartas, 25 rb: noted also by J. W. Mackail, *The Springs of Helicon,* p. 196.

suggest a poetical adaptation of Du Bartas:

> Another haunts the shore, to feed on foam:
> Another *round about the Rocks* doth roam
> *Nibbling on weeds.*   Another . . .
> . . . of *liquor only living.*   DB, 40 rb

Milton's

>   Leviathan,
> Hugest of living creatures, on the deep
> Stretched like a promontory, sleeps or swims,
> And seems a moving land, and at his gills
> Draws in, and at his trunk spouts out, a sea,   vii, 412 ff.

that leviathan which sailors "deem some island" (i, 200 ff.), re-
minds one of a passage in Du Bartas

> When on the Surges I perceive, from far,
> The Ork, Whirl-poole Whale, or huffing Physetér
> Methinks I see the wandering Isle again
> (Ortigian Delos), floating on the Main.   DB, 40 lb

But the idea is an old commonplace of natural history.[1]

Du Bartas's list of the birds and their attributes would prove a
storehouse of curiosities for readers of our own time.   Did it prove
so to Milton?

>   Part, more wise
> In common, ranged in figure, wedge their way,
> Intelligent of seasons, . . .
>
>   .   .   .   .
>
> . . . with mutual wing
> Easing their flight; so steers the prudent crane.   vii, 425 ff.

Milton's "mutual wing" is perhaps explained by Du Bartas's
words about the stork:

> Nor onely bearing them upon her back
> Through the empty Aire when their owne wings they lack.
>   DB, 45 rb

---

1. See J. H. Pitman, *Milton and the Physiologus, Modern Language Notes*, XL (1925),
439–440.

The other aspects of the wisdom of the stork and crane are much
more fully elaborated by Du Bartas than by Milton:

> the Crane . . .
> Who in the Clouds forming the forked Y,
> By the brave orders practiz'd under her,
> Instructeth Souldiers in the Art of War.
> For when her Troops of wandering cranes
>   . . . take
> Truce with the Northern Dwarfs, to seek adventure
> In *Southern Climates*.   DB, 46 lb

It will be remembered also that Milton has pygmies "warred on by
cranes"[1] but this is in *L'Image du Monde*. Milton's "crested
cock"[2] is likewise a "Crested Cock" in Du Bartas,[3] and Milton's
peacock with "starry eyes"[4] is the peacock of Du Bartas, with
"glorious eyes."[5] Du Bartas has likewise left his mark on Milton's
animals. The lion, the ounce, the libbard, the tiger[6] are all in Du
Bartas[7] (though without any special earmarks), but following
close on these come Milton's "stag" with his "branching head"
which in Du Bartas is the "Hart" "for his branched head";[8]
"fleeced the flocks"[9] in Milton echoes the "golden-fleeced sheep"
of Du Bartas;[10] the "scaly crocodile" of Milton[11] is exactly the
same "scaly Crocidile" in Du Bartas;[12] and Milton's "parsimoni-
ous emmet, *Provident* of future, in small room large heart enclosed,
Pattern of just equality,"[13] could have come from Du Bartas's:

> Thou Sluggard if thou list to learn thy part,
> Go learn the Emmets and the Urchins Art;
> In Summer the one, in Autumn th' other takes
> The Seasons fruits, and thence provision makes.[14]

---

1. *P.L.*, i, 575–576.	2. vii, 443.	3. Du Bartas, 30 lc.
4. vii, 446.	5. 46 rt.	6. vii, 464 ff.
7. 51 rb.	8. 50 rt.	9. vii, 472.
10. 50 lb.	11. vii, 474.	12. 51 rc.
13. vii, 485 ff.	14. 64 rb.	

When we come to the culminating point in the creative activities of God as emphasized strongly by both Du Bartas and by Milton, — the creation of Man, — there are unusual details in the description which indicate that Milton drew on Du Bartas. Perhaps it is of no extraordinary significance that Man is distinguished from the other creatures in both poets as follows:

> There wanted yet the *master*-work, the end
> Of all yet done, a creature who, not prone
> And brute as other creatures, but endued
> With *sanctity of reason*, might erect
> His stature, and upright with front serene
> Govern the rest, self-knowing.   vii, 505 ff.

> Yet, *not his Face down to the earth-ward bending*
> Like Beasts that but regard their belly, . . .
> . . . but towards th' Azure Skyes.
> Also thou plantedst the Intellectual Pow'r.   DB, 53 rc

Nor is it a certainty that Milton got his

> There wanted yet *the master-work*, the end
> Of all yet done   vii, 505–506

as descriptive of Man, from Du Bartas's

> All th' admirable Creatures made before,
> .   .   .   .
> Are but Essays, compar'd in every part,
> To this devinest *Master-Piece of Art*.   DB, 53 lc

But it is unusually significant in connection with these two similarities that at this particular point Du Bartas regards the creation of Man as of such importance that God the Father "consults with his onely Son," [1] and that Milton, *although God has already delegated his Son* as the actual creative agent (vii, 175), after almost three hundred and fifty lines describing the Son's creative activities, has God when he comes to the creation of Man, again *call in his son*:

1. Du Bartas, 53 lc.

> Therefore the omnipotent
> Eternal Father (for where is not he
> Present?) thus to his Son audibly spake:
> "Let *us* make now Man, in our image, Man
> In our similitude."   vii, 516 ff.

As one leaves Book vii, three general matters of some importance relating to the mass of details already mentioned need to be noticed. First, there is a glorious variety in nature. This is the principle that in part accounts for the multitudinous details of Du Bartas's and Milton's descriptions. After Milton is done with the details of creation in this book, he alludes to "variety without end."[1] Time and again he insists on the value of variety, as for example when he is describing the beauties of Paradise. Du Bartas says in regard to the details he has been relating:

> Save that the World (where one thing breeds satiety)
> Could not be fair, without so great variety.   DB, 28 rb

Secondly, and of greater importance, is the general philosophical principle announced by both Du Bartas and Milton in regard to God in his relation to all these details of his creation, — the definite declaration on the part of both, in the terms of neo-Platonism, that all these details of nature lay already full grown in the mind of God before he bodied them forth: "answering his great idea" in Milton,[2] "the idea fore-conceived" in Du Bartas.[3] Thirdly, the "immediacy" with which each group of created things respond to the voice of God is in both Milton and Du Bartas too obviously emphasized to need comment.[4] In a word, the use which Milton made of Du Bartas in Book vii is about as extensive as can well be imagined. To demand more by way of proof would be, as already suggested, to ask that Milton do in the case of Du Bartas what he never does in any case, — follow an author slavishly.

1. *P.L.*, vii, 542.   2. The same, vii, 557.   3. 140 rb.
4. See Fletcher, *Milton's Rabbinical Readings*, pp. 148 ff., for the plan of creation in Rashi and in Milton.

Book VIII

As one leaves Book vii one finds for a time a diminishing influence of Du Bartas. Several matters in Book viii which reveal Milton's use of Du Bartas material have already been indicated in connection with similar material in the earlier books. For example the "whether . . . or" formula of scientific doubt was considered in Book v, and led naturally to the consideration of the same formula used for the same purpose in Book viii.[1] But several points remain which call for mention here.

Adam continues his quest for knowledge in Book viii, pursuing his inquiry into *natural causes*. Anyone at all familiar with Du Bartas knows that more than any other poet that Milton read, Du Bartas is an inquirer into causes, at least into those causes which Adam investigates. Milton answers those inquiries in a manner more similar to Du Bartas than to any other Renaissance poet he ever had occasion to read. Like Du Bartas and many another Renaissance thinker,—Montaigne for instance,—Milton does not believe in inquiring too curiously, does not favor prying into the mystery of things as if we were God's spies. It is in Book viii[2] that he emphasizes this attitude, which, it will be remembered, is connected in Book v with the legitimate study of the *Book of God's Works*, as emphatically stressed by both Du Bartas and Milton:

> The great Architect
> Did wisely to conceal, and not divulge
> His secrets to be scanned by them who ought
> Rather admire. Or if they *list* to try
> Conjecture, he his fabric of the heavens
> Hath left to their disputes, perhaps to move
> His laughter at their quaint opinions wide
> Hereafter, when they come to model heaven
> And calculate the stars; how they will wield

---

1. viii, 70 ff.   2. 75–85.

> The mighty frame; how build, unbuild, contrive
> *To save appearances*; how gird the sphere
> With centric and eccentric scribbled o'er,
> Cycle and epicycle, orb in orb.   viii, 72 ff.

Du Bartas ridicules man's attempt to inquire unnaturally far into the unknown causes of things.[1] After enumerating many debatable issues, each introduced by the "whether . . . or" formula adopted by Milton,[2] Du Bartas adds:

> Search whoso *list*: who list let vaunt in pride
> . . . and let him, sage decide
> The many other doubts that vainly rise.
> For my own part I will not seem so wise.
>
> .   .   .   .
>
> Sith Adam's self, if now he liv'd anew,
> Could scant unwinde the knotty snarled clew
> Of double doubts and questions intricate
> That Schools dispute about this pristin state.   DB, 87 lb

And one of the subjects of the sciences (not condemned by Du Bartas in this particular instance) is described as follows:

> Informs his Phalec in the Planets course:
> What epicicle meaneth and Con-centric,
> With Apage, Perigé and Eccentrik.   DB, 142 lb

It is in Book viii also that Raphael tells Adam the relation of his little land of Eden to the wide expanse of the Heavens above him:

> And for the heaven's wide circuit, let it speak
> The Maker's high magnificence, who built
> So spacious, and his line stretcht out so far,
> *That Man may know he dwells not in his own;*
> An edifice too large for him to fill,
> Lodged in a small partition, and the rest
> Ordained for uses to his Lord best known.   viii, 100 ff.

---

1. Bacon, Montaigne, and many other Renaissance men, insist, like Horatio in *Hamlet*, that these things must not be considered too curiously, but not in language similar to Milton's.

2. See above, pp. 77 ff.

At this point is the gloss in small letters in Du Bartas [1] "Why the Lord put the man in the Garden of Eden"; the text itself reads:

> Now Heaven's . . . King
>
> .   .   .   .
>
> Thought good that man . . .
> *Should dwel elsewhere,* then where he was created;
> *That he might know, he did not hold this place*
> *By Nature's right,* but by meer gift and grace.   DB, 83 rb, 84 lt.

One other point of similarity remains to be mentioned, a trifle perhaps, but an exceedingly significant one, disclosing how small a matter in Du Bartas was sometimes remembered by Milton, and how he must have been reading him again in his latter years. God the Son describes Eve to Adam before creating her for him:

> *Thy* likeness, *thy* fit *help, thy other self,*
> *Thy* wish exactly to *thy* heart's desire.   viii, 450–451

In Du Bartas Adam calls Eve

> *His* Love, *his* Stay, *his* Rest, *his* Weal, *his* Wife,
> *His other-selfe,*[2] *his* Help.   DB, 57 rb

Another possible use of Du Bartas is Milton's allusion to the manner in which living creatures are subjugated to Adam and to be named by him:

> As *lords*
> Possess it, and all things that therein live.
>
> .   .   .   .
>
>   . . . I bring them to receive
> From thee their *names,* and pay thee *fealty*
> With low subjection; understand the same
> Of *fish within* their *watery residence.*   viii, 339 ff.

This is anticipated in Du Bartas:

> Into thy hands he put this *Monarchy;*
> Made all the Creatures know thee for their *Lord,*

---

1. P. 83 rb.
2. "My other self" (x, 128).

. . . .

> And gave thee power (as Master) to impose
> . . . *Names* unto the Hoast that rowes
> In *watery Regions*.   DB, 57 lb

In the light of the many certain details of relationship, Milton's suggestion that the Earth which Adam dwelt in before entering Paradise seemed unattractive, was probably in some sort suggested by Du Bartas:

> But when he once had entered Paradise,
> The remnant World he justly did dispise.   DB, 84 lb

Milton's Adam says:

> That what I saw
> Of Earth before scarce pleasant seemed.   viii, 305–306

Book IX

Book ix shows definitely and extensively Milton's use of Du Bartas. The discussion of Milton's conception of Satan in Book iv led logically to the consideration of Satan in his relation to Eve in Book ix. The effect of the work of Du Bartas, therefore, on Book ix up to line 779 has already received treatment in connection with Book iv.[1] The remainder of Book ix comprises another block of material of far-reaching and definite importance in relation to Du Bartas. It concerns itself in the main with the effect of the sin of Adam and Eve upon various and sundry matters related to themselves as human beings and to the whole structure and framework of the created universe. The treatment of this body of material will of necessity lead past Book ix into Book x. The scheme-work of the effect of the great transgression by Adam and Eve on Human, Animate, and Inanimate Nature is worked out by Milton to a nicety, but nicety though it may be in Milton, it had already been

1. See above, pp. 73 ff.

carried farther by Du Bartas and in almost exactly similar fashion
as to the framework and the facts of the case.[1] Milton in these two
books shows the following progressive plan of the effect of Sin.
The physical earth groans in agony at the deed. The passions enter
into the microcosmos — "the inward state" of the mind, as Milton
calls it, changes; the diseases beset man; the animals turn against
him; the Furies are let loose against him. But most significant of
all the results of Adam's Sin is the "change of Seasons" brought
about by God's shifting the earth on its axis. The first effect of Sin
is general:

> Forth reaching to the fruit, she plucked, she eat.
> Earth felt the wound, and Nature from her seat,
> Sighing through all her works, gave signs of woe.   ix, 781 ff.

When Adam eats,

> Earth trembled from her entrails, as again
> In pangs, and Nature gave a second groan.   ix, 1000–1001

Du Bartas puts this much more briefly, but the suggestion is there,
and it differs from the Biblical account:

> For, the earth feeling (even in her) th' effect
> Of the doom thundered 'gainst thy foul defect
> .   .   .   .
> With thorns and burs shall bristle up her breast.   DB, 93 lb

The last sentence of Milton's prose Argument to Book ix contains
"Eats also of the fruit. The effect thereof on them both." Du
Bartas's Argument (this is Sylvester's own term) prefacing the
Fall of Man, is as follows:

> The World's transform'd from what it was at first:
> For Adams sin, all creatures else accurst:
> Their Harmony distuned by His jar:
> Yet all againe consent, to make him war:

---

1. For the origins of this scheme and its prevalence in the Middle Ages, see above,
p. 22, note 1.

As th' Elements, and above all, the Earth:
Three ghastly Furies; Sickness, War, and Dearth.

DB, 95

Sylvester, moreover, has not gone forward twenty-seven lines before he refers to the entire change in the Universe and Man as "this woeful *alteration*." The expression "commands his Angels to make several *alterations* in the Heavens and Elements" is Milton's in his Argument to Book x. To proceed, however, with passages in Book ix after line 799 which show the use of Du Bartas material by Milton in working out his scheme of the effects of Sin on Man, the Earth, and the Cosmos. First, what both Du Bartas and Milton term the "passions" enter Adam and Eve, dethroning Reason:

Who from beneath
Usurping over *sovran Reason*, . . .   ix, 1129–1130

In Du Bartas this appears as follows:

. . . and that our Reason, there
Keeping continuall Garrison . . .
Might Avarice, Envy, and Pride subdue,

.   .   .   .

. . . that still strive to gaine
The golden Scepter from their *Soverain*.   DB, 53 rc

That Adam and Eve are conscious of guilty shame in both poets means nothing, as this comes direct from Genesis; but the effect on their general state of mind is in both poets well-nigh exactly the same.   In Milton it appears thus:

But high winds worse within
Began to rise, *high passions*, anger, hate,
Mistrust, suspicion, discord.   ix, 1122 ff.

"These sudden passions," as Du Bartas calls them in the same connection (listed by him at much greater length), follow as the effects of Adam's Sin. They are: Despair, Pride, Fear, Terror,

Shame, Ambition, "wrath and the other passions." [1] Milton proceeds to follow apparently the entire scheme of Du Bartas so minutely in regard to the effects of Adam's sin that we must trace it, in the interest of clearness, through Books x and xi.

As a result of Adam's sin, Milton proceeds to describe the alteration of the entire physical universe in order to explain the "change of seasons," [2] dangerous to man, as contrasted with the eternal Spring which both poets describe in Eden. Here, as is very rarely the case, Milton goes more into detail than Du Bartas:

>   The sun
> Had first his precept so to move, so shine,
> As might effect the Earth with cold and heat
> Scarce tolerable.   x, 651 ff.
>
>   To the winds they set
> Their corners, when with bluster to confound
> Sea, air and shore; the thunder when to roll
> With terror. . . .
> Some say he bid his Angels turn askance
> The Poles of Earth twice ten degrees and more.   x, 664 ff.
>
> These changes in the heavens, though slow produced
> Like change on sea and land, sideral blast,
> Vapour, and *mist*, and *exhalation* hot,
> Corrupt and pestilent.   x, 692 ff.

How close Milton is to Du Bartas here is obvious:

> Rebellious Adam, from his God revolting,
> Findes his yerst-subjects 'gainst himselfe insulting:
> The *tumbling* Sea, the Aire with tempests driv'n,
> Thorn-bristled Earth, the sad and low'ring Heav'n
>
> .   .   .   .
>
> Revenge on him th' Almighties injury.
> The Stars conjur'd through envious influence,
>
> .   .   .   .
>
> The Sun with heat, the Moon with cold doth vex him:
> The Aire *with unlook't-for sudden changes* checks him.
>   DB, 96 rc

---

1. Du Bartas, 100, 101.   2. *P.L.*, x, 677–678.

A thousand foggy *fumes*, which everywhere
With cloudy *mists* Heavn's crystall front besmear   DB, 96 lb

Just as impressive is the similarity in the two poets of the description of the results of Adam's Sin on the change which comes over the animals in their relation to each other and to man.   In Milton:

Beast now with beast 'gan war and fowl with fowl,
And fish with fish; to graze the herb all leaving,
Devoured each other; nor stood much in awe
Of Man.   x, 710 ff.

Nature first gave signs, impressed
On bird, beast, air — air suddenly eclipsed.
. . . Nigh in her sight
The *bird* of *Jove*, stooped from his aery tour,
Two birds of gayest *plume* before him drove;
Down from a *hill* the beast that reigns in woods
. . . pursued a gentle brace,
. . . hart and Hind.   xi, 182–189.

In exactly the same connections Du Bartas has handled many of the same details:

Since that, the Wolf the trembling Sheep pursues

.   .   .   .

And so the Princely Eagle ravening *plumes*
The feathers of all other Fowles consumes.   DB, 96 lb

One of the most extraordinary of all the borrowings by Milton from Du Bartas is his list of the Diseases [1] which fall upon man as the result of Adam's Sin:

That thou may'st know
What misery the inabstinence of Eve
Shall bring on men. . . .

.   .   .   .   .   .

. . . All maladies
Of ghastly spasm, or racking torture, qualms
Of heart-sick agony, all feverous kinds,

---

1. Raleigh, *Milton*, p. 237. See for these diseases Du Bartas, 98 ff.

Convulsions, epilepsies, fierce catarrhs,
Intestine stone and ulcer, colic pangs,
Demoniac phrenzy, moping melancholy,
And moon-struck madness, pining atrophy,
Marasmus and wide-wasting pestilence,
Dropsies and asthmas, and joint-racking rheums. xi, 475 ff.

Book X

Most of the subject matter of Book x has already been treated under Books iv and ix. Only a few scattered points in Book x remain to be considered. The first of these occurs midway in Book x in Milton's list of snakes:

Scorpion, and asp, and *amphisbæna* dire,
Cerastes horned, hydrus, and ellops drear,
And *dipsas* (not so thick swarmed once the soil
Bedropt with blood of Gorgon, or the isle
Ophiusa); but still greatest he the midst. x, 524 ff.

The following passage from Du Bartas is rather too similar to be explained on the basis of another list consulted by both poets, in the light especially of Milton's certain familiarity with so many other portions of Du Bartas: [1]

Th' innammel'd Scorpion, and the Viper-worm,
Th' *horned Cerastes*, th' Alexandrian Skink,
Th' Adder, and Drynas (full of odious stink)
Th' Eft, Snake, and *Dipsas* (causing deadly Thirst):
. . . .
Th' Amphisbena, her double banefull sting. DB, 51 lc

The next two similarities, small as they may seem in regard to the volume of their subject matter, are of extreme importance, since they form one of the very strongest links in the chain of reasoning by means of which Milton strives logically to justify on theological and common-sense grounds the ways of God to Man. Just as Adam asks:

1. Cf. Kuhns, *The Influence of Dante on Milton, Modern Language Notes*, xiii (1898), 9.

> Ah, why should all mankind,
> For one man's fault, thus guiltless be condemned?   x, 822–823

so in Du Bartas the question is put:

> O goodly Justice! one or two of us
> Have sinn'd, perhaps, and moved his anger thus;
> All bear the pain, yea even the Innocent
> Poor Birds and Beasts incurre the punishment.   DB, 114 rc

And just as Milton makes Adam say in reply to his most difficult question for God to answer in justifying his ways to Man,

> Inexplicable
> Thy justice seems.   Yet, to say truth, *too late*
> I thus contest; *then should have been refused*
> *Those terms whatever, when they were proposed.*
> *Thou did'st accept them.*   x, 754 ff.

So Du Bartas states the idea, that Man, having entered into "those terms" with God, should be willing as a matter of contract to take the bad with the good. Du Bartas [1] makes God propose the exact terms of this contract to Adam, makes Adam accept it, and then has Adam add:

> I honour in my soule, and humbly kisse
> Thy just Edict (as Author of my blisse):
> Which, once transgrest, deserves the rigour rather
> Of sharpest Judge, then mildnesse of a Father.   DB, 85 rt

One small matter remains at the very end of Book x, where Milton interests us in the partly utilitarian and material problem of Adam thrown up against unfriendly Nature and meeting with his defenseless body the hardships of a world now at enmity with man:

> And teach us further by what means to shun
> The inclement seasons, rain, ice, hail, and snow!
> Which now the sky with various face begins
> To show us in this mountain, while the winds
> Blow . . .

1. P. 85 lc.

> . . . which bids us seek
> Some better shroud, some better warmth to cherish
> Our limbs benumbed, ere this diurnal star
> Leave cold the night, how we his gathered beams
> Reflected, may with *matter sere* foment,
> Or by collision of *two bodies* grind
> The *air attrite* to fire; as *late the clouds*,
> *Justling* or pusht with *winds*, rude in thir shock,
> *Tine* the *slant lightning*, whose thwart flame, driven down,
> *Kindles* the gummy bark of *fir or pine*,
> And sends a comfortable heat from far,
> Which might supply the sun.   x, 1062 ff.

Now Du Bartas is very much more interested in this matter than Milton, but there are details in his description which Milton apparently found to his liking. Adam is described almost as a Robinson Crusoe, meeting each emergency with inventive genius. He cannot live comfortably without Fire:

> Yet fire they lackt; but lo, *the winds* that whistle
> Amid the Groves, so oft the *Laurell* justle
> Against *the Mulberry*, that their angry claps
> Do *kindle fire*.   DB, 105 lb

Again, when Adam, hunting, hurls a flint stone at his quarry, but misses, and sees the flint hit rock and the sparks fly, —

> In his left hand a *shining flint he locks*,
> Which with another in his right he knocks   DB, 105 rc

until the sparks ignite the dry leaves. It is all the more probable that Milton is indebted to Du Bartas here as in the passage which immediately follows this in Du Bartas, where he is describing the origin of the mechanic arts with Cain and Tubal Cain, we have one of the most unescapable of all the passages which have served as sources for Milton. But this carries us over into Book xi.

Book XI

Book xi stands out conspicuously as drawing very extensively upon the *Divine Weekes*. Nowhere in *Paradise Lost* is the indebtedness more absolutely clear. In connection with the Books already considered we have found it necessary to take up certain portions of Book xi. In considering the Effects of Sin on Adam's race, for example, it was necessary to cite the lists of diseases which in both poets are given in the same connection and in similar language. The Milton list comes in this book. The matters now to be considered are therefore only a part of the evidence as to what Milton found interesting in Du Bartas in building up Book xi. They almost all occur in that section which deals with Adam's being allowed to see in a vision, and to have foretold to him, those events of Biblical history which show the varying fortunes of his descendants, culminating in the Redemption of Mankind through the Second Adam, Christ. The interpretation of these events for the most part shows the moral failure of Adam's race. Occasionally, as in the case of Noah, there is a moral success. Probably no more extraordinary case of epic compression is to be found than in the last two books of *Paradise Lost* where Milton passes before us in swift review these events of Biblical history. But this compression becomes even more marvellous if it is regarded in its true relation to the facts of the case, as a handling of the Biblical events tremendously elaborated by Du Bartas. The last half of Book xi and the first half of Book xii narrate these events in less than one thousand lines; Du Bartas covers the same set of events in fifteen thousand lines, narrating the events of Biblical history in *The Divine Weekes* from *The Handicrafts* to *The Decay*. Some of the traces of Du Bartas in this part of Milton's work are therefore rather slight, but many of them are so obvious as to require no comment.

These events of the Old Testament are thrown into the same setting in Milton as in Du Bartas. That is to say, they are most of them seen in a vision by Adam and regarded as prophetic.[1] In both poets they serve the purpose of arousing the sensations of terror and pity in Adam and are followed by a series of comments by him. His comments, in both Milton and Du Bartas, take the form of exclamations of pity, fear, and condemnation. In Du Bartas the exclamations are all in one passage. Milton employs them more dramatically, bringing them in at intervals, each after some dismal disclosure. Other aspects of this matter have been taken up in Book vii.[2]

The first of the visions in Milton is Cain's murder of Abel. There is little if any influence of Du Bartas here. Perhaps it is worth noting that Cain, in both Milton and Du Bartas, kills Abel with a stone; and that Milton's description of Abel as "rolling in dust and gore" [3] may be due to Du Bartas's "The murdered face lies printed in the mud." [4] There is also the word "sweaty," used by Milton of Cain (xi, 434) and used by Milton nowhere else. Was it suggested by "sweating Tubal stands" [5] in a passage of Du Bartas which follows immediately after his account of Cain? This passage, at all events, had caught Milton's eye, for his account of Tubal Cain in the second of the visions which Michael allows to pass before the eyes of Adam, shows clearly the influence of Du Bartas. In Milton this vision concerns itself mainly with Tubal as the discoverer of metals in the earth and as the inventor of the mechanic arts and of musical instruments. The Du Bartas materials which helped to build up the Miltonic vision are:

---

1. See also E. C. Baldwin, *Paradise Lost and the Apocalypse of Moses, Journal of English and Germanic Philology*, xxiv (1925), 383–386. Cf. pp. 89 ff., above.
2. Pp. 90 ff., above.   3. *P.L.*, xi, 460.
4. P. 106.
5. P. 107 rb.

While through a Forrest Tubal . . .
. . . did a Boar pursue, . . .
A burning Mountain from his *fiery vain*
An *yron River rowls along the Plain*:

.   .   .   .

And first perceiving, that this scalding mettle,
Becomming cold, in any shape would settle,
And grow to hard. . . .

.   .   .   .

He casts a hundred plots, and yer ye parts
He moulds the ground-work of a hundred Arts:

.   .   .   .

In *two square creases of unequel sises*
To *turn to iron streamlings he devises*;
Cold takes them thence: *then off the dross he rakes,*
And this an Hammer, that an Anvill makes;

.   .   .   .

And grown more cunning, hollow things he formeth,

.   .   .   .

Then beats a Blade, and then a Lock invents.

.   .   .   .

While (compast round with smoaking Cyclops
Half-naked Bronts, and Sterops swarthy-hewd,
All well-neer weary) *sweating Tubal stands,*
Hastning the hot work in their sounding hands,
No time lost Jubal: th' *un-full Harmony*
Of *uneven Hammers, beating diversly,*
Wakens the tunes that his sweet numbery soule
Yer birth (some think) learn'd of the warbling Pole.

DB, 107 lt

Compare Milton:

He looked, and saw a spacious *plain,* whereon
Were tents of various hue; by some were herds
Of cattle grazing; others, whence *the sound*
Of instruments that *made melodious chime*
Was heard, of harp and organ, and *who moved*
Their stops and *chords was seen: his volant touch*
Instinct through all proportions, low and high,
Fled and pursued transverse the resonant fugue.
In other part *stood one who, at the forge*
Labouring, two massy clods of iron and brass

Had melted (whether found where casual fire
Had *wasted woods, on mountain* or in vale,
Down to the veins of Earth, thence gliding hot
To some caves mouth, or whether washed by stream
From underground); the liquid ore he drained
Into *fit moulds prepared*; from which he formed
First his own tools; then, what might else be wrought
Fusil or graven in metal.   xi, 556 ff.

Nigh on the *plain*, in *many cells* prepared,
That underneath had veins of liquid fire
Sluiced from the lake, a second multitude
With wondrous art found out the massy ore,
Severing each kind, and *scummed the bullion-dross.*
A third as soon had formed within the ground
A various mould, and from the boiling cells
By strange conveyance *filled each hollow nook*:
As in an organ, from one blast of wind,
To many *a row of pipes* the *sound-board breathes.* . . . .   i, 700 ff.

It is important to notice that, immediately after the Tubal Cain
description just quoted, Du Bartas returns to Adam. After in-
structing Seth in knowledge, the Adam of Du Bartas falls into a
trance, like Adam in Milton, and, as in Milton, sees the vision of
the future. Du Bartas narrates, though much more briefly in these
particular visions, many of the same facts of Biblical history that
Milton likewise visualizes for the reader in Adam's trance in Book
xi. The other episodes which he uses in Books xi and xii he gets
from the Du Bartas books which immediately follow. The close
proximity of the two preceding Du Bartas blocks of material deal-
ing with the origin of the mechanic arts and music to the Du
Bartas passage that views the future through Adam's trance, is
significant, and becomes particularly so when we observe that two
additional pieces of material in Adam's vision in Du Bartas are
strikingly similar to the two next pieces of material to be considered in Milton's vision. These are the Flood episode, and the
marriage of the Hebrews with pagan women resulting in the race of
cruel giants. Milton's borrowing from Du Bartas's episode of the

Flood is so indisputably clear that it makes practically certain the conclusion that Milton was aided by Du Bartas in the entire framework of Books xi and xii. Du Bartas's description of the Flood is swift and graphic:

> Heav'ns chrystall windows with one hand he opes,
> Whence on the World a thousand Seas he drops:
> With th' other hand he gripes and wringeth forth
> The spungy Globe of th' execrable Earth,
> So straightly prest, that it doth straight restore
> All liquid floods that it had drunk before:
> In every Rock new Rivers doe begin;
> And to his ayd the snowes come tumbling in:
>
> . . . .
>
> The shores do shrink, the swelling waters grow.
> Alas! so many Nephews lose I here.
>
> . . . .
>
> I should be seed-lesse: but (alas!) the Water
> Swallows those Hils, and all this wide Theater
> Is all one Pond.   O Children, whither fly-you?
> Alas! Heav'ns wrath pursues you to destroy-you:
> The stormy Waters strangely rage and roar,
> Rivers and *Seas have all one common shore*,
> (To wit) a *Sable, water-loaden Sky*,
> Ready to rain new Oceans instantly.   DB, 109 rb.

From this passage it will shortly be shown that Milton got suggestions. It is well to notice at this point, however, that Du Bartas is here repeating in varied form the account of the Flood which appeared toward the beginning of his work, at the end of the Second Day of the First Weeke,[1] where he is describing the creation of water after the creation of land. By what process he drifted here into a description of Noah's Flood, which of course comes much later in the history of the world, I am not prepared to say. Singularly enough *there are two descriptions* of the Flood *in Milton likewise* and only sixty-eight lines apart, a repetition unexampled among all other descriptions of the visions shown to Adam in these

---

1. Du Bartas, 18, 19.

last two books of *Paradise Lost*. The first Du Bartas description is in part to be found at the end of the Second Day of the First Weeke.[1] The passages obviously related to Du Bartas will be commented upon in detail.[2] A few of the more important follow. In Milton the south wind plays an important part in organizing the storm, as in Du Bartas:

> Meanwhile the *south-wind* rose, and with black *wings*
> Wide hovering, all the *clouds* together drove
> From under heaven.   xi, 738 ff.

Du Bartas begins thus:

> And let loose *Auster*, and his lowring race
> . . . with drooping *wing*;
>
> .   .   .   .
>
> And both their hands, wringing thick *clouds* asunder.
>   DB, 19 lt

In both Du Bartas and Milton the earth, like the heavens, contributes its share of the moisture:

> Hills, to their supply,
> Vapour, and exalation, dusk and moist
> *Sent up* amain.   xi, 740 ff.

Du Bartas has it:

> The earth shakes for fear and sweating doth consume her
> And in her veins leaves not a drop of humor.
>   DB, 19 lc

Even the splendid imaginative touch of Milton —

> Sea covered sea,
> *Sea without shore*, and in their *palaces*,
> *Where* luxury late reigned, *sea monsters* whelped
> And stabled.   xi, 749 ff.

---

1. The same.
2. *P.L.*, xi, 738–752, 818–833, 840–854.

owes something to Du Bartas:

> The Sturgeon, coasting over *Castles*, muses
> (Under the Sea) to *see so many houses*.
> The Endian Manat, and the Mullet float
> O'r Mountain tops, *where* erst *the bearded Goat*
> Did bound and brouz: DB, 19 lb

Milton's "sea without shore" occurs in the same connection in Du
Bartas: "Now the Ocean hath no shore." [1] Perhaps the most extraordinary of all the parallels is Milton's "made the flowing of the
fresh wave shrink" and Du Bartas's "wave into wave did sink,
with sudden speed all rivers gan to shrink." This suddenness of the
beginning and end of the Flood in both Du Bartas and Milton is not
at all suggested by Genesis. In Milton the waters are a "*standing
Lake*" [2]; in Du Bartas, "a *standing* Gulf" [3] and "all one *Pond*." [4]
Of prime importance is the use by Milton of Du Bartas's idea of
the storm as controlled rather mechanically by "sluices":

> Who now had *stopt*
> His *sluices*, as the *heaven* his windows *shut*.   xi, 848–849

> Now *stopping* close the . . . Fountains
> *Shutting Heav'ns sluces*.   DB, 116

The fact that Paradise is referred to by both poets [5] as being
swept away by the Flood, though in a different context, makes
their two treatments of the Flood all the more interesting to compare. In the passage describing the Flood at the very end of the
Handy-Crafts [6] Du Bartas's "Heav'ns chrystall windows with one
hand he opes" is of course improved by Milton in "as the heavens
his windows shut." Michael says [7] "A *world* devote to *universal
wrack*," and Adam exclaims in Du Bartas,[8] as he sees the end of the

---

1. See Du Bartas quotation, p. 116: "Seas have all one common shore . . . a water-
loaden sky." This is from Ovid, Metamorphoses, i, 292.

2. *P.L.*, xi, 847.   3. Du Bartas, 19 l.   4. 109 rb.

5. xi, 829–832; Du Bartas, 83 lc.

6. Du Bartas, 109.   7. xi, 821.   8. Du Bartas, 109.

Flood (quoted above), "O *world's* decay! O *Universall wrack.*" He has already in the Du Bartas passage cried out in his agony at the sight, "O *children*, whither fly you"; so in the Milton passage:

> O visions ill foreseen!
>
> . . . . .
>
>   Let no man seek
> Henceforth to be foretold what shall befall
> Him or his *children.*   xi, 763, 770 ff.

 One other certain borrowing from Du Bartas remains before we proceed to gather up the other details which look strongly in the direction of Du Bartas. In reading the long and highly colored elaboration by Du Bartas of the wanderings and wars of the Hebrews which makes up the bulk of his epic, Milton had found the following rendition of one of the narrative bits there presented, and he had found it *only six lines before Du Bartas's description of the Flood*; and Milton reproduces it *only thirty lines before his own description of the Flood*:

> The sacred Flock . . .
>
> . . . . . .
>
> With lustful eyes choosing for wanton spouses
> Mens wicked daughters . . .
>
> . . . .
>
> From these profane, foul, cursed kisses sprung
> A cruell brood, feeding on bloud and wrong;
> Fell *Gyants* strange, *of haughty hand and minde,*
> *Plagues of the World, and scourges of Mankinde.*   DB, 109
>
> To whom thus Michael: These are the product
> Of those ill-mated marriages thou saw'st;
> Where good with bad were matched, who of themselves
> Abhor to join; and, by imprudence mixed,
> Produce prodigious births *of body or mind.*
> Such were these *Giants*, men of high renown;
>
> . . . . . .
>
> *Destroyers* rightlier called and *plagues of men.*   xi, 683 ff.

The remaining material of Book xi which has been affected apparently by the narrative of the wanderings of the Hebrews before they reach the promised land of Canaan could never be presented in such fashion as to make certain the fact that Milton is here borrowing from Du Bartas, but this book of *Paradise Lost* and the first few hundred lines of Book xii would afford study for anyone interested in following a probability. A careful perusal of Du Bartas's last books would yield fruitful results as to the departures of Du Bartas in these books from the Biblical renderings of the same events as compared with Milton's departures. Two blocks of material of Du Bartas in these books have had a fairly certain effect on Milton. The first is the Du Bartas treatment of the Plagues of Pharaoh.[1] It is interesting to note that in this case Du Bartas, like Milton, condenses instead of elaborating, but that where they do expand, occasionally their phrases are similar. For example, the locusts in Du Bartas are referred to as a "cloud" and they "swarm." Neither word is in the Bible; both are in Milton.

Of much more significance is the treatment of the wars of wandering Hebrew tribes in Book xi and in Du Bartas, in view of the treatment in recent years by scholars of Milton's knowledge of the art of war.[2] Milton himself knew something of the art of war from his personal experience. But it will be admitted that Du Bartas knew more. He served in a position of great importance and had seen the horrors of war beyond the experience of most men of letters in any age. He had been wounded, and the sight of blood and wounds was to him a first-hand experience. His interest therefore, in military manœuvers, tactics, and technical terms, and in graphic pictures of the ghastly side of war, is extremely natural, and is made manifest by the unusual elaboration which these matters receive in the books above referred to, where he often di-

1. Du Bartas, 169; *P.L.*, xii, 176–192.
2. J. H. Hanford, *Milton and the Art of War, Studies in Philology*, XVIII (1921), 232 ff.

gresses in this regard. It would be difficult to find any other epic
writer who has ever gone so much into detail in depicting the hor-
rible and disgusting side of battles. He revels in ghastly details. If
one reads the pertinent passages in the *Divine Weekes* and then
turns to those portions of Book xi and xii of *Paradise Lost* which
touch upon the revolting aspects of war, one may well conclude
that Du Bartas here also left his mark on Milton.

Book XII

At the very beginning of Book xii Michael, perceiving that
Adam's faculties are growing faint under the strain of actually beholding in a vision the unhappy experiences of his descendants, culminating in the Flood which destroys mankind, proceeds to narrate directly the history of mankind from the Flood to Judgment
Day. Within a very few lines the Du Bartas influence begins to
make itself manifest. In his account of Nimrod, the first episode of
Book xii, Milton, like Du Bartas, strongly emphasizes Nimrod's
tyranny and his absurd audacity in attempting to build in such
fashion as to rival God. How similar the two accounts are becomes
immediately obvious as soon as they are placed in close proximity:

Milton	Du Bartas
Till one shall rise,	Yer Nimrod had attained to . . .
Of proud, ambitious heart, who . . .	years
. . . . . .	He *tyranniz'd* —
Will . . .	. . . .
. . . quite dispossess	
Concord and law of Nature from the Earth;	*Leaves hunting Beasts*, and *hunteth Men.*
Hunting (*and men, not beasts shall be his game*)	
. . . .	This *Tyrant*
	DB, 120
He, with a crew, whom like ambition joins	quoth he . . .
	. . . . .

With him or under him to *tyrannize,*[1]

.   .   .   .

. . . shall find
The plain, wherein a black bituminous
    gurge
Boils out from under ground, the mouth
    of Hell;
Of brick, and of that *stuff,* they cast to
    build
A city and tower . . .
And get themselves a name, *lest,* far
    dispersed
In foreign lands, thir *memory* be lost.

.   .   .   .

But *God* . . .

.   .   .   .

. . . *them beholding soon,*
Comes down . . .
. . . and in derision sets
Upon thir tongues a various spirit . . .

.   .   .   .

To sow a *jangling noise.*   xii, 24 ff.

Lets found a City . . .

.   .   .   .   .

                              for fear
Lest sever'd thus . . . .
We be *disperst* . . .

.   .   .   .   .

. . . let's leave *memorials*
Of our great names . . .

.   .   .   .   .

Here . . . heap they . . .
The *gummy slime* . . . of waters
There busy *Kil-men* ply . . .
For *brick* and tyle . . .
They dig to Hell.[2]

.   .   .   .   .   .

Which God perceiving . . .

.   .   .   .   .

. . . soon confousedly did bound
Through   all   the   worke . . . strange
    sound,
A *jangling noise.*

                              DB, 120, 121

There can be no doubt that the beginning of Book xii was affected by the beginning of Du Bartas' *Babalon.*[3] Du Bartas leads up to his account of Nimrod by a discourse on tyranny. He attacks tyrants, boldly bringing it all home to France:

> Print (O Heav'ns King!) in our King's heart a zeal
> First, of thy lawes; then of their public weal.   DB, 120 lt

Milton weaves into his account of Nimrod his attack on tyranny and follows the Nimrod episode with a more direct attack, bringing it likewise home, though without mentioning England by name:

1. This is the only example of *tyrannize* in all Milton's poetry. Cf. the second line quoted from Du Bartas.

2. See "to hell they dig" in the same connection in Candy, *Milton-Ovid Script, Some Newly Discovered Stanzas written by John Milton,* London 1924, p. 74.

3. P. 121.

> Yet sometimes nations will decline so low
> From virtue, which is reason, that no wrong,
> But justice and some fatal curse annexed,
> Deprives them of their outward liberty.   xii, 97 ff.

Though applying this to the "irreverant son of Noah," Milton doubtless had in mind England's return to Charles II after her freedom from kings under Cromwell. The rest of the Nimrod episode in Milton is too similar to Du Bartas to be explained by the assumption of a common source as yet undiscovered. Both poets refer to Nimrod's *hunting not Beasts but Men*; both describe the strange stuff (associated in both with hell) out of which the building materials are made; [1] both build the Tower out of "Brick" and a second "stuff"; both assign as the reason for building the city and tower the fact that the people are no longer to be "disperst," using this identical term; and both assign as additional the reason that the memory of their tribe shall not be lost.

From this point on in Book xii the other striking episodes in the wanderings and wars of the Hebrews recounted by Michael, though embodying much of the matter of Du Bartas (contained in *The Colonies, The Columnes, The Vocation, The Fathers, The Law, The Captains*), are so tremendously condensed as compared with Du Bartas that the evidence of influence is very slight. The crossing of the Red Sea in both is of substantial and sentimental interest, as one detail, clear and unmistakable in Du Bartas, which had made its impression on Milton as a boy of fifteen, still holds its fascination for him as a man past fifty:

> And on each side is flanked all along
> With *Wals of Crystall*, beautiful and strong.
>
> .   .   .   .
>
> Two *Wals of Glasse*, built with a word alone.   DB, 171 lc

This descriptive detail of the sides of the lane through the Red Sea

---

1. See for Milton's and Du Bartas's views against mining, G. C. Taylor, *Modern Language Notes*, XLV (1930), 24.

made by God for the Israelites to pass in safety had already appeared in Milton's metrical version of Psalm 136:

> The flood stood still like *Walls of Glass*, —

one of the few Du Bartas touches conceded by scholars as an early influence. Here in Book xii this the earliest of Milton's borrowings becomes again the last concrete borrowing in *Paradise Lost*:

> As on dry land, between *two crystal walls*.   xii, 197

The other accounts by Milton of the events of Hebrew history, when read in connection with Du Bartas's lengthy renderings of the same material, afford the reader perhaps his best opportunity to observe Milton's wonderful compression of Du Bartas. Possibly he had in mind the defects of the enormously detailed method of presentation of Du Bartas when he says, or has Michael say,[1]

> The rest
> Were long to tell: how many battles fought;
> How many kings destroyed and kingdoms won;
> Or how the sun shall in mid-heaven stand still.   xii, 260 ff.

For all these matters are recounted by Du Bartas on a far more elaborate scale than in the Bible. Nowhere else can one get a truer sense of the contrast between the artistry of Milton and the pedestrian quality of Du Bartas than in these very matters.

To close, however, in that vein, would be only to echo once more the traditional cry as to the worthlessness of Du Bartas and Sylvester, repeated already often enough by many who apparently have read neither with any great degree of care. It is to be hoped rather that one about whom Goethe, the greatest of modern poets, and Sainte Beuve,[2] the greatest of modern critics, speak with respect and admiration, and upon whom the greatest of English poets since Shakespeare leaned in so intimate a fashion, will not continue to be of interest mainly as a fit subject for the exercise of raillery and superficial wit.

1. Suggested by W. R. Abbot.
2. *Tableau de la Poésie Française au XVIe Siècle*, Paris 1869, pp. 380 ff.

BIBLIOGRAPHY

Bibliography

ABBOT, W. R., *Studies in the Influence of Du Bartas in England, 1584–1641.* MS. dissertation, University of North Carolina, 1931.

AGAR, HERBERT, *Milton and Plato,* Princeton University Press, 1928.

ASHTON, H., *Du Bartas en Angleterre,* Paris, 1908.

BAILEY, MARGARET LEWIS, *Milton and Jakob Boehme,* New York, 1914.

BALDWIN, EDWARD CHAUNCEY, *Milton and Plato's Timæus, Publications of the Modern Language Association,* XXXV (1920), 210 ff.

—— *Paradise Lost and the Apocalypse of Moses, Journal of English and Germanic Philology,* XXIV (1925), 383 ff.

BARHAM, FRANCIS, *Adamus Exul of Grotius, or The Prototype of Paradise Lost,* London, 1839.

BRUCE, J. DOUGLAS, *Campailla, Berkeley and Milton, The Nation,* New York, XCVII (1913), 32–33.

BUNDY, M. W., *Milton's View of Education in Paradise Lost, Journal of English and Germanic Philology,* XXI (1922), 127 ff.

CANDY, HUGH C. H., *Milton's Early Reading of Sylvester, Notes and Queries,* CLVIII (1930), 93–95.

—— *Some Newly Discovered Stanzas written by John Milton on Engraved Scenes illustrating Ovid's Metamorphoses.* London [1924].

Du Bartas, His Divine Weekes and Workes, translated by Joshua Sylvester, Gent., London, 1641.

EDMUNDSON, GEORGE, *Milton and Vondel,* London, 1885.

FLETCHER, HARRIS FRANCIS, *Contributions to a Milton Bibliography, 1800 to 1930,* University of Illinois Press, Urbana, 1931.

—— *Milton's Rabbinical Readings,* University of Illinois Press, Urbana, 1930.

GILBERT, ALLAN H., *Milton and the Mysteries, Studies in Philology,* XVII (1920), 147 ff.

GOOD, JOHN Walker, *Studies in the Milton Tradition,* University of Illinois Press, Urbana, 1915.

GREENLAW, EDWIN, *The New Science and English Literature in the Seventeenth Century, The Johns Hopkins Alumni Magazine,* XIII (1925), 331 ff.

—— *Spenser's Influence on Paradise Lost*, Studies in Philology, XVII (1920), 320 ff.

—— *A Better Teacher Than Aquinas*, Studies in Philology, XIV (1917), 196 ff.

HAIGHT, THERON WILBER, editor, *The Divine Weeks of Joshua Sylvester*, Waukesha, Wisconsin, 1908.

HANFORD, JAMES HOLLY, *The Pastoral Elegy and Milton's Lycidas*, P.M.L.A., XXV (1910), 403 ff.

—— *A Milton Handbook*, F. S. Crofts & Co., New York (revised), 1933.

HARTWELL, KATHLEEN ELLEN, *Lactantius and Milton*, Harvard University Press, Cambridge, 1929.

KUHNS, OSCAR, *The Influence of Dante on Milton*, Modern Language Notes, XIII (1898), 1 ff.

LANHAM, LOUISE, *Hymnic Elements in Milton's Poetry*, MS. dissertation, University of North Carolina, 1927.

LARSON, MARTIN A., *Milton and Servetus*, P.M.L.A., XLI (1926), 891 ff.

LAUDER, WILLIAM, *An Essay on Milton's Use and Imitation of the Moderns in his Paradise Lost*, London, 1750.

LEE, SIR SIDNEY, *The French Renaissance in England*, Oxford, 1910.

MACKAIL, JOHN WILLIAM, *The Springs of Helicon*, New York, 1909.

MERRILL, ROBERT VALENTINE, *The Platonism of Joachim Du Bellay*, University of Chicago Press, 1925.

Monthly Mirror, X (1800), 155–156.

MOODY, WILLIAM VAUGHN, *The Complete Poetical Works of John Milton*, Boston, 1924.

MÜNCH, WILHELM, *Die Enstehung des Verlorenen Paradieses*, Cleve, 1874.

NICOLSON, MARJORIE H., *The Spirit World of Milton and More*, Studies in Philology, XXII (1925), 433 ff.

—— *Milton and Hobbes*, Studies in Philology, XXIII (1926), 405 ff.

—— *Milton and The Conjectura Cabbalistica*, Philological Quarterly, VI (1927), 1 ff.

NORLIN, GEORGE, *The Conventions of the Pastoral Elegy*, American Journal of Philology, XXXII (1911), 294 ff.

PELLISSIER, GEORGES, *La vie et les œuvres de Du Bartas*, Paris, 1883.

PITMAN, JAMES HALL, *Milton and the Physiologus*, Modern Language Notes, XL (1925), 439–440.

POMMRICH, EWALD, *Milton's Verhältnis zu Torquato Tasso*, Halle, 1902.

PRIOR, OLIVER HERBERT, editor, *L'Image du Monde de Maître Gossouin, Redaction en Prose*, Lausanne, 1913.

—— Caxton's *Mirrour of the World*, E.E.T.S., Extra Series, CX, 1913.

PRITCHARD, J. P., *The Influence of the Fathers Upon Milton, with Especial Reference to St. Augustine*. MS. dissertation, Cornell University, 1925.

RALEIGH, WALTER, *Milton*, London, 1900.

ROBBINS, FRANK EGLESTON, *The Hexaemeral Literature, a Study of the Greek and Latin Commentaries on Genesis*, University of Chicago Press, 1912.

SAURAT, DENIS, *Milton, Man and Thinker*, London, 1925.

—— *Milton and the Zohar*, Studies in Philology, XIX (1922), 136 ff.

STERN, ALFRED, *Milton und Seine Zeit*, London, 1877.

STEVENS, DAVID HARRISON, *A Reference Guide to Milton from 1800 to the Present Day*, University of Chicago Press, 1930.

STEVENSON, HAZEL ALLISON, *Herbal Lore as Reflected in the Works of the Major Elizabethan Poets and Dramatists*. MS. dissertation, University of North Carolina, 1930.

SYLVESTER, JOSHUA, *Du Bartas, His Divine Weekes and Workes*, London, 1641.

TASSO, TORQUATO, *Le Sette Giornate del Mondo Creato*, Milan, 1608.

THIBAUT DE MAISIÈRES, MAURY *Les Poèmes Inspirées du Début de la Genèse à l'Epoque de la Renaissance*, Louvain, 1931.

THOMPSON, ELBERT N. S., *Essays on Milton*, Yale University Press, 1914.

TILLYARD, EUSTACE M. W., *Milton*, London, 1930.

UPHAM, ALFRED HORATIO, *The French Influence in English Literature, from the Accession of Elizabeth to the Restoration*. Columbia University Press, New York, 1908.

VERITY, ARTHUR WILSON, *Paradise Lost*, Cambridge University Press, 1921.

WILLIAMS, GEORGE G., *The Beginnings of Nature Poetry in the Eighteenth Century*, Studies in Philology, XXVII (1930), 583 ff.